The Twelve Powers of Man

BY CHARLES FILLMORE

Sixth Edition

UNITY SCHOOL OF CHRISTIANITY

KANSAS CITY, MO.

1941

Introduction

JESUS prophesied the advent of a race of men who
would sit with Him on twelve thrones, judging
the twelve tribes of Israel. This book explains
the meaning of this mystical reference, what
and where the twelve thrones are, and what attain-
ments are necessary by man before he can follow
Jesus in this phase of his regeneration. Regeneration
follows generation in the development of man. Generation sustains and perpetuates the human; regeneration unfolds and glorifies the divine.

It is not expected that beginners in the study of
metaphysical Christianity will understand this book.
It deals with forces that function below and above
the field of the conscious mind. The average religious
thinker knows nothing about the subconscious mind
and very little about the superconscious; this book
presupposes a working knowledge of both.

This book aims to clear up the mystery that ever
envelops the advent, life, and death of Jesus. To the
superficial reader of the Gospels His life was a
tragedy and, so far as concerns the kingly reign that
was prophesied, it was a failure. Yet those who
understand the subtlety of the soul and the supremacy of Spirit see that Jesus was conqueror of a psychic
force that was destroying the human race.

Jesus was the star actor in the greatest drama ever
played on earth. This drama was developed in the
celestial realm, its object being to inject new life into

perishing men. The full significance of this great plan of salvation cannot be understood by man until he awakens faculties that relate him to the earth beneath and the heavens above.

It has long been prophesied that the time was ripe for the advent on this planet of a new race, and there has been much speculation as to the character and advent of the superman. Herein is set forth the metaphysical idea of the spiritual quickening of man on the human plane and his transformation into the divine: not by a miracle or the fiat of God, but by the gradual refinement of the man of flesh into the man of Spirit. As Paul taught, "This corruptible must put on incorruption, and this mortal must put on immortality."

Jesus was the "first-fruits" of those who are coming out of the mortal into the immortal. He was the type man, the Way-Shower, and, through following His example and taking on His character as a spiritual-minded man, we shall come into the same consciousness.

Spiritual discernment always precedes demonstration, consequently more is taught in this book as a possibility of attainment by man than has been demonstrated by any man save Jesus. Those who feel that they are ready for the great adventure in the attainment of eternal life in the body here and now should not be deterred because there are no outstanding examples of men who have risen to this most exalted degree. Through mental energy, or the dynamic power of the mind, man can release the life

4

of the electrons secreted in the atoms that compose the cells of his body. Physical science says that if the electronic energy stored in a single drop of water were suddenly released its power would demolish a six-story building. Who can estimate the power stored in the millions of cells that compose the human body? The method of release of this body energy and its control are mystically taught by Jesus. He was transfigured before His disciples, "and his face did shine as the sun, and his garments became white as the light." Before His crucifixion He had attained such mastery over His body cells that He told the Jews that they might destroy His body and "in three days" He would "raise it up." He demonstrated this in the resurrection of His body after it had been pronounced lifeless. When He disappeared in a cloud He simply unloosed the dynamic atoms of His whole body and released their electrical energy. This threw Him into the fourth dimension of substance, which He called the "kingdom of the heavens."

The dynamic energy that man releases through prayer, meditation, and the higher activities of his mind is very great, and, if not controlled and raised to the spiritual plane, may prove a source of body destruction; if carried to the extreme, it may even prove a cause of soul destruction. "Be not afraid of them that kill the body, but are not able to kill the soul: but rather fear him who is able to destroy both soul and body in hell." This one who is able to destroy both soul and body in Gehenna is the personal self or selfish ego in man.

The electronic energy in man is a form of fire, which is represented by Gehenna. This electronic fire must be used unselfishly. If used to further the selfishness of man it becomes destructive, through the crosscurrents that it sets up in the nervous system.

We do not encourage those who still have worldly ambitions to take up the development of the twelve powers of man. You will be disappointed if you seek to use these superpowers to gain money (turn stones into bread), control others ("the kingdoms of the world . . . All these things will I give thee"), or make a display of your power ("If thou art the Son of God, cast thyself down"). These are the temptations of the selfish ego, as recorded in the 4th chapter of Matthew, which Jesus had to overcome, and which all who follow Him "in the regeneration" have to overcome.

Unspeakable joy, glory, and eternal life are promised to those who with unselfish devotion strive to develop the Son of God consciousness. All the glories of the natural man are as nothing compared with the development of the spiritual man. The things of this world pass away, but the things of Spirit endure forever. In his flesh body man may be compared to the caterpillar that is the embryo of the butterfly. In its undeveloped state the caterpillar is a mere worm of the earth, but it has, infolded within it, a beautiful creature awaiting release from its material envelope. Paul visualized this when he wrote in Romans 8:22, "For we know that the whole creation groaneth and travaileth in pain together until now. And not only so, but ourselves also, who have the first-fruits of the Spirit, even we ourselves groan within ourselves, waiting for *our* adoption, . . . the redemption of our body."

Jesus, the Great Teacher, gave many lessons for our instruction, the greatest and most mystical being the Book of Revelation. Here He showed Himself to John as He is in His redeemed body. He stood in the midst of seven lights, which represent the seven ideas of Divine Mind ruling in the restored earth. "One like unto a son of man, clothed with a garment down to the foot, and girt about at the breasts with a golden girdle. And his head and his hair were white as white wool, *white* as snow; and his eyes were as a flame of fire; and his feet like unto burnished brass, as if it had been refined in a furnace; and his voice as the voice of many waters. And he had in his right hand seven stars: and out of his mouth proceeded a sharp two-edged sword: and his countenance was as the sun shineth in his strength."

This description of the appearance of Jesus is partly symbolical, because John did not himself understand the full import of the powers that were being exercised by the spiritual man, whose words were so clean-cut that they appeared to John as a two-edged sword; whose eyes were so discerning that they seemed a flame of fire; whose voice was like the rippling of many waters. Language is poor and bare when one seeks to describe the glories of

7

the spiritual state. Comparisons within the comprehension of the reader are necessary, and they but tamely tell of the superhuman man and his powers.

However, this pen picture by John of what he saw when he was lifted up "in the Spirit on the Lord's day" gives us a glimpse of what the redeemed man is like, and what we shall attain when we "awake, with thy likeness."

It should be thoroughly understood that this sight of Jesus that was given to John was not a vision of a man who had died and gone to a heaven up in the skies, but it was the opening of John's eyes to existence in what may be termed the fourth-dimension man. We use this term *fourth dimension* because it is the name given to a state of existence that popular material science says must be, in order to account for the effects that are being expressed on every side. It is also called the interpenetrating ether, which is not to be understood as something material, or as being matter, but as something having properties far more substantial than matter. Through the application of mathematical principles scientific men are proving the existence of the spiritual side of Being. This does not refer to the psychical realm in which undeveloped souls rest while awaiting reincarnation. Many people take it for granted that soul realms and spiritual realms are identical. But these stand to each other as moonshine and sunshine. Jesus called the interpenetrating state of being the kingdom of heaven, or, in the original Greek, "the kingdom of the heavens." He said that it was like a treasure hid in a field, which, when a man discovered it, he would sell all that he had to buy. The majority of Christians believe that they are going to this heaven when they die, but Jesus does not teach that the dead go first to glory. On the contrary, Jesus teaches that death may be overcome. "If a man keep my word he shall never see death." Paul taught that Jesus attained victory over death. "Christ being raised from the dead dieth no more." "Let not sin therefore reign in your mortal body, that ye should obey the lusts thereof: neither present your members unto sin *as* instruments of unrighteousness; but present yourselves unto God, as alive from the dead, and your members *as* instruments of righteousness unto God."

The Psalmist writes:

"What is man, that thou art mindful of him?
And the son of man, that thou visitest him?
For thou hast made him but little lower than God,
And crownest him with glory and honor.
Thou makest him to have dominion over the works
        of thy hands;
Thou hast put all things under his feet."

With the mind of the seer, Ralph Waldo Emerson says:

"Great hearts send forth steadily the secret forces that incessantly draw great events, and wherever the mind of man goes, nature will accompany him, no matter what the path."

9

Verily I say unto you, that ye who have followed me, in the regeneration when the Son of man shall sit on the throne of his glory, ye also shall sit upon twelve thrones, judging the twelve tribes of Israel. And every one that hath left houses, or brethren, or sisters, or father, or mother, or children, or lands, for my name's sake, shall receive a hundredfold, and shall inherit eternal life.

—JESUS

CONTENTS

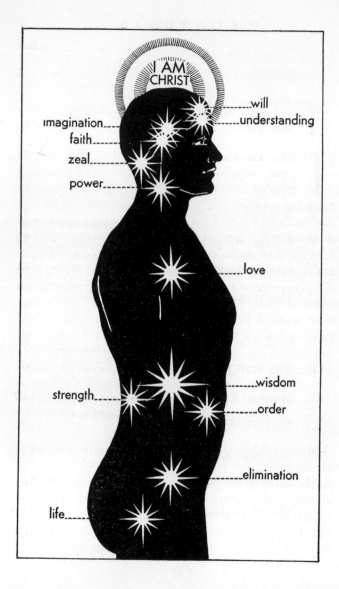

CHAPTER I

The Twelve Powers of Man

THE subconscious realm in man has twelve great centers of action, with twelve presiding egos or identities. When Jesus Christ had attained a certain soul development, He called His twelve disciples to Him. This means that when man is developing out of mere personal consciousness into spiritual consciousness, he begins to train deeper and larger powers; he sends his thought down into the inner centers of his organism, and through his word quickens them to life. Where before his powers have worked in the personal, now they begin to expand and work in the universal. This is the first and the second coming of Christ, spoken of in the Scriptures. The first coming is the receiving of Truth into the conscious mind, and the Second Coming is the awakening and the regeneration of the subconscious mind through the superconscious or Christ mind.

Man expands and grows under divine evolution as an industrial plant grows. As the business expands, it is found that system is necessary. Instead of one man's being able to do the work with the assistance of a few helpers, he requires many helpers. Instead of a few helpers, he needs hundreds; and in order to promote efficiency he must have heads for the various departments of the work. Scripture symbology calls the heads of departments in man's consciousness the twelve disciples.

Each of these twelve department heads has control of a certain function in soul or body. Each of these heads works through an aggregation of cells that physiology calls a "ganglionic center." Jesus, the I AM or central entity, has His throne in the top head, where phrenology locates spirituality. This is the mountain where He so often went to pray. The following outline gives a list of the twelve disciples, the faculties that they represent, and the nerve centers at which they preside:

Faith—Peter—center of brain.

Strength—Andrew—loins.

Discrimination or Judgment—James, son of Zebedee—pit of stomach.

Love—John—back of heart.

Power—Philip—root of tongue.

Imagination—Bartholomew—between the eyes.

Understanding—Thomas—front brain.

Will—Matthew—center front brain.

Order—James, son of Alphaeus—navel.

Zeal—Simon the Cananaean—back head, medulla.

Renunciation or Elimination—Thaddaeus—abdominal region.

Life Conserver—Judas—generative function.

The physiological designations of these faculties are not arbitrary—the names can be expanded or changed to suit a broader understanding of their full nature. For example, Philip, at the root of the tongue, governs taste; he also controls the action of the larynx, as well as all vibrations of power throughout the organism. So the term "power" expresses but a small part of his official capacity.

The first disciple that Jesus called was Peter. Peter represents faith in things spiritual, faith in God. We begin our religious experience, our unity with Divine Mind, by having faith in that mind as omnipresent, all-wise, all-loving, all-powerful Spirit.

Faith in the spiritual man quickens spiritual understanding. Peter believed that Jesus was the Messiah; his faith opened his spiritual discernment, and he saw the living Christ back of the personal mask worn by Jesus. When asked, "Who do men say that the Son of man is?" the disciples, looking upon personality as the real, said: "Some *say* John the Baptist; some, Elijah; and others, Jeremiah, or one of the prophets." Then Jesus appealed to their own inner spiritual understanding and He said: "But who say ye that I am?" Only Simon Peter answered: "Thou art the Christ, the Son of the living God." And Jesus answered, "Thou art Peter, and upon this rock I will build my church, and the gates of Hades [the grave] shall not prevail against it. I will give unto thee the keys of the kingdom of heaven."

Spiritual discernment of the reality of man's origin and being is the only enduring foundation of character. It was to this faith in the understanding of the real being of man that Jesus gave power in earth and heaven. It was not to the personal Peter that Jesus gave the keys to His kingdom, but to all

17

THE TWELVE POWERS OF MAN

who through faith apply the binding (affirming) and loosing (denying) power of Spirit in the earth (substance consciousness). Right here and now the great work of character-building is to be done, and whoever neglects present opportunities, looking forward to a future heaven for better conditions, is pulling right away from the kingdom of heaven within himself.

People who live wholly in the intellect deny that man can know anything about God, because they do not have quickened faith. The way to bring forth the God presence, to make oneself conscious of God, is to say: *I have faith in God; I have faith in Spirit; I have faith in things invisible.* Such affirmations of faith, such praise to the invisible God, the unknown God, will make God visible to the mind and will strengthen the faith faculty. Thus the faith disciple (Peter) is called and instructed spiritually.

When a center loses its power it should be baptized by the word of Spirit. We are told in the Scriptures that Philip went down to Gaza ("the same is desert"), and there baptized a eunuch. Gaza means a "citadel of strength." It refers to the nerve center in the loins, where Andrew (strength) reigns. "Lo now, his strength is in his loins." Gaza is the physical throne of strength, as Jerusalem is the throne of love.

The back grows weak under the burden of material thought. If you are given to pains in your back, if you become exhausted easily, you may know at once that you need treatment for freedom from material burdens. Eliminate from your mind all thought of the burdens of the world, the burdens of your life, and all seeming labors. Take your burdens to Christ. "Come unto me, all ye that labor and are heavy laden, and I will give you rest."

We are pressed upon by ideas of materiality. Thoughts make things, and the material ideas that are pressing upon us are just as substantial in the realm of mind as material things are substantial in the realm of matter. Everything has origin in thought, and material thoughts will bring forth material things. So you should baptize and cleanse with your spiritual word every center, as Philip baptized the eunuch of Gaza. Baptism is cleansing. It always represents the erasing power of the mind.

When the baptizing power of the word is poured upon a center, it cleanses all material thought; impotence is vitalized with new life, and the whole subconsciousness is awakened and quickened. The word of the Lord is there sown in the body, and once the word of the Lord is sown in any of these centers—the cells of which are like blank phonograph records—they take the thought that is given them, and send it through the whole organism. The baptism of strength goes to the uttermost parts of the body, and every one of the twelve disciples, under the divine law, feels the new strength.

James, the son of Zebedee, represents discrimination and good judgment in dealing with substantial things. James is the faculty in man that wisely chooses and determines. It may be in the matter of food; it may be in the matter of judgment about the relation of external forces; it may be in the choosing of a wife or a husband—in a thousand different ways this faculty is developed in man. The spiritual side of the James faculty is intuition, quick knowing.

James and John are brothers, and Jesus called them "sons of thunder." These brothers preside over the great body brain called the solar plexus, or sun center. James has his throne at the pit of the stomach; and John, just back of the heart. They are unified by bundles of nerves and are metaphysically closely related. Whatever affects the stomach will sympathetically affect the heart. People with weak stomachs nearly always think they have heart trouble.

Jesus Christ called those two disciples "sons of thunder" because of the tremendous vibrations or emotions that go forth from the solar plexus. When your sympathies are aroused, you will find that you begin to breathe deeply and strongly, and if you are very sympathetic you can feel the vibrations as they go out to the person or thing to which you are directing your thought. All fervor, all the high energy that comes from soul, passes through these centers.

Bartholomew represents the imagination. The imagination has its center of action directly between the eyes. This is the point of expression for a set of tissues that extend back into the brain and connect with an imaging or picture-making function near the root of the optic nerves. Through this faculty you can project an image of things that are without, or

20

ideas that are within. For instance, you can project the image of jealousy to any part of your body and, by the chemistry of thought combined with function, make your complexion yellow, or you can image and project beauty by thinking goodness and perfection for everybody. Bartholomew is connected directly with the soul, and has great power in the pictures of the mind. Jesus saw him under a fig tree, a long way off, before he was visible to the natural eye. Do not imagine anything but good, because under the law of thought combined with substance it will sooner or later come into expression, unless you head it off, eliminate it by denial.

Man has faculties of elimination, as well as of appropriation. If you know how to handle them you can expel error from your thought body. The denial disciple is Thaddaeus, presiding in the abdominal region, the great renunciator of the mind and the body. All the faculties are necessary to the perfect expression of the man. None is despised or unclean. Some have been misunderstood; through ignorance man has called them mean, until they act in that way and cause him pain and sorrow. The elimination, by Thaddaeus, of the waste of the system through the bowels is a very necessary function.

Thomas represents the understanding power of man. He is called the doubter because he wants to know about everything. Thomas is in the front brain, and his collaborator, Matthew, the will, occupies the same brain area. These two faculties are jointly in occupation of this part of the "promised land." Like the land of Ephraim and Manasseh, their inheritance is undivided.

James, the son of Alphaeus, represents divine order. His center is at the navel.

Simon, the Cananaean, represents zeal; his center is at the medulla, at the base of the brain. When you burn with zeal and are anxious to accomplish great things, you generate heat at the base of your brain. If this condition is not balanced by the co-operation of the supplying faculties, you will burn up the cells and impede the growth of the soul. "For the zeal of thy house hath eaten me up."

Judas, who betrayed Jesus, has his throne in the generative center. Judas governs the life consciousness in the body, and without his wise co-operation the organism loses its essential substance, and dies. Judas is selfish; greed is his "devil." Judas governs the most subtle of the "beasts of the field"—sensation; but Judas can be redeemed. The Judas function generates the life of the body. We need life, but life must be guided in divine ways. There must be a righteous expression of life. Judas, the betrayer of Jesus, must in the end be cleansed of the devil, selfishness; having been cleansed, he will allow the life force to flow to every part of the organism. Instead of being a thief (drawing to the sex center the vital forces necessary to the substance of the whole man) Judas will become a supplier; he will give his life to every faculty. In the prevailing race consciousness Judas drains the whole man, and the body dies as a result of his selfish thievery.

22

It is through Judas (the desire to appropriate and to experience the pleasure of sensation) that the soul (Eve) is led into sin. Through the sins of the sex life (casting away of the precious substance), the body is robbed of its essential fluids and eventually disintegrates. The result is called death, which is the great and last enemy to be overcome by man. Immortality in the body is possible to man only when he has overcome the weaknesses of sensation, and conserves his life substance. When we awaken to the realization that all indulgence for pleasure alone is followed by pain, then we shall know the meaning of eating of the tree of the knowledge of good and evil, or pleasure and pain.

If you would build up your faculties under the divine law, redeem Judas. First have faith in the power of Spirit, and then speak to Judas the word of purity. Speak to him the word of unselfishness; baptize him with the whole Spirit—Holy Spirit. If there is in you a selfish desire to exercise sensation, to experience the pleasures of sense in any of its avenues, give that desire to the Lord; in no other way can you come into eternal life.

These twelve powers are all expressed and developed under the guidance of Divine Mind. "Not by might, nor by power, but by my Spirit, saith Jehovah of hosts." You must keep the equipoise; you must, in all the bringing forth of the twelve powers of man, realize that they come from God: that they are directed by the Word of God, and that man (Jesus) is their head.

CHAPTER II

The Development of Faith

FAITH has an abiding place in man's consciousness. This place of abiding is described in the Scriptures as the "house of Simon and Andrew." A house is a structure that some person has built for a home. A man's house is his castle. Perhaps generation after generation is born and reared in the same house. The house where a great genius was born is preserved with care, and it is visited year after year by those who are devotees of the one who expressed some great thought, art, or discovery. If the barn cave at Bethlehem, where Jesus was born, were found, it would become the most famous shrine in the world. The importance that we give to the places where great men and women were born is founded on the centralizing power of thought. All structures are thought concentrations. Constructive thinking ultimates in the construction of places of abode. Savages do not build houses or cities, because they do not think constructively.

In the time of David the Children of Israel were nomads. The consciousness of indwelling Spirit had not been born in their minds, and could not, in consequence, be formed in their bodies. That the time was ripe for a more constructive state of mind is set forth in these words of Jehovah, in II Samuel 7:5, 6:

Shalt thou build me a house for me to dwell in? for

24

I have not dwelt in a house since the day that I brought up the children of Israel out of Egypt, even to this day, but have walked in a tent and in a tabernacle.

After receiving this message, David, the drawing power of love, began gathering material for Solomon's Temple. Jehovah told David that he could not build the Temple because he was a man of war. The temple of God is man's body ("Your body is a temple of the Holy Spirit"), but if man has not complied with the law of permanent body building, he is like the nomadic Children of Israel; he goes from body to body and from tabernacle to tabernacle.

> Except Jehovah build the house,
> They labor in vain that build it.

The tents and the tabernacles that the Children of Israel built for Jehovah represent the transitory bodies of flesh. The Lord has merely "walked" in these flimsy temples; they have not afforded an abiding place for Spirit, because of their unsubstantial character. The underlying weakness of the tent body was its lack of faith in the inhabiting soul. A new consciousness of the indwelling spiritual substance and life in the soul was necessary, and a man was chosen to bring it forth. This man, named Abraham, represents obedience and faith. His original name was Abram, which means "exalted father." The name is identified with the highest cosmic principle, the all-pervading, self-existent spiritual substance, which is the primary source of the universe.

Abraham was tested again and again, to the end

25

that his soul might be strong in faith. His great test of faith was his willingness to sacrifice his beloved son, Isaac, in the mountain of the Lord. "And Abraham called the name of that place Jehovah-jireh: as it is said to this day, In the mount of Jehovah it shall be provided."

This incident is intended to show the necessity of the soul's giving up that which it considers its dearest possession before it can realize the divine providence. The incident takes place in the mount of the Lord; that is, in a high spiritual understanding.

The law of giving and receiving pertains to the realm of ideas; one must give up personal attachments before one can receive the universal. If a parent idealizes a child, loves it so dearly that its pleasure is first in his consciousness, the spiritual development of the parent is impeded. Then, before the love of God (which is the supreme thing) can fill the heart, there must be a sacrifice of human love. If like Abraham one is faithful and obedient and willing to give to the Lord his most precious possession, there is always a receiving or providing equivalent.

When Abraham was willing to sacrifice his beloved Isaac, the Lord stayed his hand; his attention was directed to a ram in a thicket near by, and he was directed to sacrifice the animal upon the altar, in place of the child. Here is illustrated an often misunderstood law of sacrifice or renunciation. We do not have to give up our cherished things, if they are real, but the error that prevents their full expression must be destroyed. The ram (which represents the resistance and opposition of personality to the complete expression of Truth) must be sacrificed.

"Give, and it shall be given unto you" is the statement of a law that operates in every thought and act of man. This law is the foundation of all barter and financial exchange. Men scheme to get something for nothing; but the law, in one of its many forms, overtakes them in the end. Even metaphysicians, who above all people should understand the law, often act as if they expected God to provide abundantly for them before they have earned abundance. It is an error to think that God gives anybody anything that has not been earned. The Holy Spirit comes upon those who pray in the "upper room." The "upper room" corresponds to the "mount of Jehovah." It is the high place in consciousness where man realizes the presence of Divine Mind. The greatest work that one can do is to strive to know God and to keep His law. God pays liberally for this service and the reward is sure. Faith is built up in consciousness under this law.

"Faith is assurance of *things* hoped for." When there has been an aspiration and a reaching out for the spiritual life, the faith faculty becomes active in consciousness. The prayer of supplication is impotent—the prayer of affirmation is immediately effective.

Intellectual faith admits doubt, and hope of fulfillment in the future; spiritual faith includes unfailing

assurance and immediate response. These two attitudes of faith are often observed acting and reacting
upon each other. Peter started to walk on the water
in spiritual faith, but when he saw the effects of the
wind he was afraid, and began to sink. Then the
I AM (Jesus) gave its hand of spiritual power, the
wind ceased, and there was no longer any doubt of
faith's ability to rise above the negative consciousness.

The first and greatest disciple of Jesus was Peter,
who has been universally accepted by the followers
of Jesus the Christ as a type representing faith. Before he met Jesus this disciple was called Simon.
Simon means "hearing," which represents receptivity.
We understand from this that listening to Truth in
a receptive state of mind opens the way for receiving
the next degree in the divine order, which is faith.
Jesus gave Peter his new name and also its meaning:
"Thou art Peter, and upon this rock I will build my
church."

Faith in the reality of the invisible builds a real,
abiding substance in mind and in body. All kinds
of ideas grow quickly when planted in this rich
substance of the mind. Jesus also called this substance of faith the "earth," and He said to Peter,
"Whatsoever thou shalt bind [affirm] on earth shall
be bound in heaven; and whatsoever thou shalt loose
[deny] on earth shall be loosed in heaven." In all
His teaching Jesus emphasized that the ruling forces
of both heaven and earth are in man. "The kingdom
of God is within you." "All authority hath been
given unto me in heaven and on earth." "Is it not

written in your law, I said, Ye are gods?" When we understand the omnipresence of Spirit (God) we quickly see how simple and true this beautiful doctrine of Jesus is.

There is but one real faith; the avenue of expression determines the character and power of faith. Trust is a cheaper brand of faith, but trust is better than mistrust. As a rule, people who merely trust in the Lord do not understand all the law. If they had understanding they would affirm the presence and power of God until the very substance of Spirit would appear in consciousness—and this is faith established on a rock.

Faith words should be expressed both silently and audibly. The power of the spoken word is but slightly understood, because the law of the Word is not rightly observed. The Word is the creative idea in Divine Mind, which may be expressed by man when he has fulfilled the law of expression. All words are formative but not all words are creative. The creative Word lays hold of Spirit substance and power. Physical science hints at this inner substance and energy, in its description of the almost inconceivable power inherent in the universal ether. We are told that the manifest forces, such as heat, light, and electricity, are but faint manifestations of an omnipresent element which is thousands of times greater than these weak expressions.

Radio is opening up a new field of activity in the use of the spoken word. A newspaper article on the wireless telephone says:

Do you happen to know that a single word spoken in lower Broadway, New York, among the skyscrapers, could break every pane of glass in adjacent buildings and create a disturbance that would be felt for a mile in every direction?

The human voice, transformed into electrical energy for wireless transmission, develops 270 horse power. The power of ten men is equal to one horse power. The human voice electrified for wireless purposes is equivalent to the power of 2,700 men. In the various processes that step up a voice for radio transmission across the Atlantic ocean, it becomes 135,000 times more powerful than when uttered by the person sending the message.

Thus, starting with an initial energy of 1/1,000 of an electric watt, the voice is boosted by a powerful station until it is intensified 100 million times.

If the spoken word can be mechanically intensified a hundred million times, how much greater will be its power when energized by Spirit! When Jesus said with a loud voice to Lazarus, "Come forth," He must have made contact with the creative Word referred to in the 1st chapter of John, because the results showed its life-giving character. When He healed the centurion's servant by His word sent forth on invisible currents, He said that the work was done through faith. So faith must boost the spoken word even more than a hundred million times, as evidenced by its marvelous results. That the word of faith has an inner force, and that this force rushes forth and produces remarkable transformations in the phenomenal world, is the testimony of thousands who have witnessed its results.

Jesus said: "If ye have faith as a grain of mustard seed, ye shall say unto this mountain, Remove hence to yonder place; and it shall remove; and nothing shall be impossible unto you." He knew about the great spiritual machinery that the word of faith sets into action. He illustrated how man spiritually developed could by faith control the elements, quell storms, walk on water, retard or increase the growth of life and substance in grains, trees, animals, and men.

The ponderous dynamos that generate electricity to light a city are set going by a touch on a button. There is a button in the mind of man that connects him, through faith, with almighty energy. When the word of faith is spoken to large tumors and they melt away, is not the transformation equal to the removal of mountains? When a paralyzed limb, or a lifeless organ, is quickened and restored to natural functioning, is not that quickening a raising of the dead?

It is not necessary that the one who touches the button of faith shall understand all the intricate machinery with which he makes contact; he knows, like one who turns the electric switch, that the light or power will spring forth. The faith center, the pineal gland, opens the mind of man to spiritual faith. Merely affirming the activity of this super-power will quicken it in consciousness. Jesus said, "I speak not from myself: but the Father (faith) abiding in me doeth his works."

The transformers of electricity are paralleled by the transforming power of mind. That if a man sanely believes he can do a thing he will eventually find a way to do it is an accepted axiom of psychology. The mind generates an energy that contacts the universal energy, and causes circumstances and events to fall into line for the attainment of the latent ideal. John came crying in the wilderness of mortal thought, "Repent ye"; that is, change your mind. Paul discerned a like necessity, hence his call: "Be ye transformed by the renewing of your mind."

When people see the possibilities that follow a right change of mind, they will crowd the halls of metaphysical teachers as they now crowd moving-picture shows. When it is clearly understood that doubt, fear, poverty, disease, and death—every thought, good or bad, that men have expressed—have existence through mind we shall see a shifting of consciousness and a radical change in thought and word by everybody of sane mind. Then we shall ask for the true source and find it, as did Paul, who said: "Have this mind in you, which was also in Christ Jesus." It was not Jesus but the mind in Jesus that did the great works. He was the center of faith that transformed the mighty creative forces of Being (which are active in the universe through the mind and brain of man) into a form of force usable in His environment. Tap this inner reservoir of faith, and you can do what Jesus did. That was His promise; its fulfillment is the test of a true follower.

"By faith Enoch was translated that he should not see death . . . By faith Noah . . . prepared an ark to the saving of his house . . . By faith Abraham, being tried, offered up Isaac . . . By faith Moses, when he was born, was hid three months by his parents . . . By faith the walls of Jericho fell down . . . And what shall I more say? for the time will fail me if I tell of Gideon, Barak, Samson, Jephthah; of David and Samuel and the prophets: who through faith subdued kingdoms, wrought righteousness, obtained promises, stopped the mouths of lions, quenched the power of fire, escaped the edge of the sword, from weakness were made strong, waxed mighty in war, turned to flight armies of aliens. Women received their dead by a resurrection."

Chapter III

Strength—Stability—Steadfastness

"WHEN the strong *man* fully armed guardeth his own court, his goods are in peace: but when a stronger than he shall come upon him, and overcome him, he taketh from him his whole armor wherein he trusted, and divideth his spoils."

Jesus gave the forgoing illustration of a strong man's being overcome by a stronger. The incident is mentioned in three of the Gospels, those of Matthew, Mark, and Luke. It is usually interpreted as illustrating in a general way the overcoming of evil, but the peculiar identification of the strong man in his court (or house), and the necessity of overcoming him, hint at a deeper significance. One who has studied man as an aggregation of personalities readily identifies the "strong man" as one of the twelve foundation powers or disciples that make up the manifest man. Among the disciples of Jesus the strong man is designated as Andrew, brother of Peter. The Greek meaning of Andrew is "strong man."

The development of the natural world from coarser to finer types in vegetable life and in animal life is paralleled in many respects in the unfoldment of man. The source of everything is in the realm of ideas; a knowledge of this fact, coupled with faith in the working power of the unseen, makes man greater than all other expressions of Divine Mind. However, knowledge of the law of mind evolution does not relieve man of the necessity of refining and transmuting the various types of man that he has brought forth, and of which he is the epitome.

The Jehovah man is constantly making the Adam man and breathing into his nostrils the breath of life. The Adam man exists in the subconsciousness as a multitude of men: The wise man and the foolish man, the kind man and the cruel man, the loving man and the hateful man, the stingy man and the generous man, the hungry man and the full man, the happy man and the troubled man, the weak man and the strong man, the good man and the bad man, the live man and the dead man, the poor man and the rich man, the timid man and the courageous man, the sick man and the healthy man, the old man and the young man, the erratic man and the sane man—these, and a thousand other types of man as active personalities, occupy the consciousness of every human being. Every male has within him the female and every female has within her the male. This fact is admitted by physiology, substantiating the Genesis record of the ideal creation of man as "male and female," and his expression in Adam and Eve as the male and female in one man. The fact was corroborated by the Great Teacher when He said, "Have ye not read, that he who made *them* from the beginning made them male and female?"

The "strong *man* fully armed," referred to by

Jesus, is the strength and stability in man. In the natural man he is manifest as physical strength, but in the regeneration he is overcome and his possessions are divided or given to the other faculties as a nucleus around which the higher forces gather. The "stronger than he" who takes away the "whole armor" in which the strong man trusted is spiritual strength. The overcoming of Goliath by David illustrates the mastery of the spiritual over the material. Goliath trusted in his armor, which represents the protective power of matter and material conditions. David, spiritual strength, had no armor or material protection. David's power was gained by trust in divine intelligence, through which he saw the weak place in Goliath's armor. Direct to this weak place, with the sling of his concentrated will, he sent a thought that shattered the forehead of the giant. This incident shows how easy it is to overcome the seemingly strong personal and material conditions when the mind of Spirit is brought into action.

David was sure of himself, because he had slain the lion that had killed his sheep. The lion is the beast in man; when overcome, or, rather, transmuted to finer energy, this lion becomes a mighty soul strength.

The life of Samson, as set forth in Judges, shows the different movements of strength in human consciousness, and its betrayal and end. Samson did all kinds of athletic stunts, but was finally robbed of his strength by Delilah, a Philistine woman, who had his head shaved while he slept on her knees. Hair represents vitality. When the vital principle is taken away the strength goes with it. The body is weakened by this devitalization and finally perishes. Eve took away the strength of Adam in like manner, and every man who gives up the vital essence of his body for the pleasure of sensation blindly pulls down the pillar of his temple, as did Samson.

Supreme strength as demonstrated by Jesus can be attained by one who trusts in Spirit and conserves his vital substance. The strength of Spirit is necessary to the perpetuation of soul and body and to the overcoming of death. "For there are eunuchs, that were so born from their mother's womb: and there are eunuchs, that were made eunuchs by men: and there are eunuchs, that made themselves eunuchs for the kingdom of heaven's sake."

The body has many "brain" and nerve centers, through which the mind acts. Consciously we use only the brain in the head. We should think through every cell in the organism, and consciously direct every function in building up the body. When one has attained the mastery of these various bodily functions through thinking in the brain center that stores the vital energy of each particular faculty, then all deterioration ceases and the body is perpetually renewed.

The strength here discussed is not physical strength alone, but mental and spiritual strength. All strength originates in Spirit; and the thought and the word spiritually expressed bring the manifestation. "The name of Jehovah is a strong tower."

We grow to be like that which we idealize. Affirming or naming a mighty spiritual principle identifies the mind with that principle; then all that the principle stands for in the realm of ideas is poured out upon the one who affirms.

"Be strong in the Lord, and in the strength of his might" is a great strengthening affirmation for ourselves and for others. Be steadfast, strong, and steady in thought, and you will establish strength in soul and in body. Never let the thought of weakness enter your consciousness, but always ignore the suggestion and affirm yourself to be a tower of strength, within and without.

The development of man is under law. Creative mind is not only law, but it is governed by the action of the law that it sets up. We have thought that man was brought forth under the fiat or edict of a great creative mind that could make or unmake at will, or change its mind and declare a new law at any time; but a clear understanding of ourselves and of the unchangeableness of Divine Mind makes us realize that everything has its foundation in a rule of action, a law, that must be observed by both creator and created.

Man's development is not primarily under the physical law, because the physical law is secondary. There is a law of Spirit, and the earthly is but the showing forth of some of the results of that law. We begin our existence as ideas in Divine Mind; those ideas are expressed and developed and brought to fruitage, and the expression is the important part of the soul's growth.

Evolution is the result of the development of ideas in mind. What we are is the result of the evolution of our consciousness, and that consciousness is the result of seed ideas sown in our mind. When Froebel, the great teacher of children, began his primary school, he thought a long time before he gave it a name. One day the name came to him, "a children's garden"; so he called his school a "kindergarten." Froebel may not have seen the connection, but in naming his system of educating the children of men, he was true to the plan given in Genesis 2:8. Humanity is the garden of God, of which the soil is the omnipresent thought substance.

Jesus says that the seed is the word; He gives illustrations of the various places in which the seed is sown, and the results of the sowing. The seed, or Word of God, is sown in the minds of men; these seed ideas go through many changes, and they bring forth a harvest according to the capacity of the receiving soil. If you will to do the will of God, the exercise of your will in God-Mind strengthens your will power. If you have faith in things invisible, the faith seed is growing in your mind and your faith will be increased. Every word or idea in Divine Mind is sown by man in his mind, and is there brought forth—according to man's receptivity. "Whatsoever a man soweth, that shall he also reap." So all the faculties that exist in Divine Mind (the twelve pillars of the temple of God) are in this way expressed through the soul and the body of man.

Some have claimed that the Bible is a work on physiology. So it is, but it is far more; it treats of spirit, soul, and body as a unit. That is the reason why those who have studied the Bible from a merely physiological standpoint have not understood it. They have looked for descriptions of flesh and bones. In truth those things have no active existence without accompanying life and intelligence; and the Bible sets forth this fact in many symbols.

Jesus Christ, the Great Teacher, who knew what was in man, began His evolution with Spirit. He is the "only begotten Son of God"; He is the type that you should strive to follow, not only in spiritual culture and in soul culture, but in physical culture. If you would bring forth the very best that is in you, study the methods of Jesus Christ. Study them in all their details, get at the spirit of everything that is written about this wonderful man, and you will find the key to the true development of your soul and your body. If you will carry out His system, there will be revealed to you a new man, a man of whom you never dreamed, existing in the hidden realms of your own subconsciousness.

CHAPTER IV

~~~

Wisdom—Judgment

WHICH is the greater, wisdom or love? After long study of the analysis of love given by Paul in the 13th chapter of I Corinthians, Henry Drummond pronounced love to be "the greatest thing in the world." His conclusion is based on Paul's setting forth of the virtues of love. Had wisdom been as well championed as love was, the author of "The Greatest Thing in the World" might not have been so sure of his ground. It goes without argument that love wins when everything else fails, but, notwithstanding her mightiness, she makes many blunders. Love will make any and every sacrifice for the thing that she loves; on the other hand, she is enticed into trap after trap in her blind search for pleasure. It was this kind of love that caused Eve to fall under the spell of sensation, the serpent. She saw that the fruit of the tree was "pleasant to the eyes." She followed the pleasure of life instead of the wisdom that would have shown her how to use life. Ever since we have had pleasure and pain, or good and evil, as the result of Eve's blind love.

What kind of people would we be if Eve and Adam had been obedient to the Lord of wisdom, instead of obeying the sense of love? This is one of the biggest questions that any one can ask. It has been debated for many, many centuries. It has a double answer. Those who get the first answer will claim that it is correct, and those who get the second answer will assure you that there can be no other conclusion. The question hinges on one point, and that is: Must one experience evil in order to appreciate good? If it were possible for man to know all the wisdom and joy of the Infinite, he would have no necessity for experience with the opposite. But do we have to have pain before we can enjoy pleasure? Does the child that burns its hand on a hot stove have a larger consciousness of health when the hand is healed? Has it learned more about stoves? Unnumbered illustrations of this kind might be given to show that by experimentation we learn the relations existing between things in the phenomenal world. But if we apply this rule to sciences that are governed by absolute rules, it becomes evident that there is no necessity for knowing the negative. To become proficient in mathematics it is not necessary that one make errors. The more closely one follows the rules in exact sciences, the more easily and successfully one makes the demonstrations. This goes to prove that the nearer one comes to the absolute or cause side of existence, the greater is one's understanding that wisdom and order rule, and that he who joins wisdom and order rules with them.

God knows that there is a great negative, which is a reflection of His positive, but He is not *conscious* of its existence. We know that there is an underworld of evil, in which all the rules of civilized life are broken, but we are not *conscious* of that world because we do not enter into it. It is one thing to view error as a thing apart from us, and quite another to enter into consciousness of it. In the allegory of Adam and Eve, the man and the woman were told by wisdom not to "eat" (not to enter into consciousness of the fruit of the tree of knowledge of good and evil). But the pleasure of sensation (serpent) tempted them, and they ate.

Sensation, feeling, affection, and love are closely allied. Sensation is personified in the Edenic allegory as the serpent, the most subtle of the beasts of the field (animal forces alive in substance). The subtlety of sensation in its various guises is in its pleasure, the thrill that comes when mind and matter join in the ecstasy of life. When the desire for the pleasures of sensation is indulged and the guiding wisdom ignored, a realm of consciousness is established that regards the material universe as the only reality. The Lord, the knowing side of man, talks to him in the "cool of the day." In the heat of passion and the joy of pleasure, man does not listen to the "still, small voice," but in the "cool of the day," that is, when he cools off, he reflects, and he hears the voice of wisdom and judgment saying: "Where art thou, Adam?"

The "great day of judgment"—which has been located at some fateful time in the future when we all shall be called before the judge of the world and have punishment meted out to us for our sins

—is every day. The translators of the Authorized Version and of the American Standard Version of the New Testament are responsible for the "great judgment day" bugaboo. In every instance where judgment was mentioned by Jesus, He said "in a day of judgment," but the translators changed *a* to *the,* making the time of judgment appear a definite point in the future, instead of the repeated consummations of causes that occur in the lives of individuals and nations. We know that we are constantly being brought to judgment for transgressing the laws moral and physical. Yet back of these is the spiritual law, which the whole race has broken and for which we suffer. It was for the mending of this broken law that Jesus was incarnated.

When we awaken to the reality of our being, the light begins to break upon us from within and we know the truth; this is the quickening of our James or judgment faculty. When this quickening occurs, we find ourselves discriminating between the good and the evil. We no longer accept the race standards or the teachings of the worldly wise, but we "judge righteous judgment"; we know with an inner intuition, and we judge men and events from a new viewpoint. "Knowledge comes but wisdom lingers," sings the poet. This pertains to intellectual development only. When man kindles the inner light, he speaks the word of authority to his subjective faculties. Jesus represents the Son-of-God consciousness in man, to whom was given dominion over all the earth. The Son-of-God man is wholly spiritual, and he uses spiritual thoughts, words, and laws in all that he does.

When Jesus called His disciples, He spoke silently to the faculties that preside over and direct the functions of mind and body. When He called Peter, James, and John, there was in His consciousness a quickening of faith, judgment, and love. These three disciples are mentioned more often than His other disciples because they are most essential in the expression of a well-balanced man. Andrew (strength) was also among the first few called; he represents the stability that lies at the foundation of every true character.

"James the Just" was the title bestowed by historians upon the first bishop of Jerusalem. There were many Jameses among the early followers of Jesus, and there is some doubt as to whether James the Just and James the disciple are identical.

An analysis of man in his threefold nature reveals that on every plane there is a certain reflective and discerning power of the mind and its thoughts. In the body, conclusions are reached through experience; in intellect, reason is the assumed arbiter of every question; in Spirit, intuition and inspiration bring the quick and sure answer to all the problems of life. Jesus was the greatest of the teachers of men, because He knew all knowledge from the highest to the lowest. He did not blight the senses by calling them "error" (because they are limited in their range of vision), but He lifted them up. He took Peter, James, and John up into the mountain, and was trans-

45

figured before them. When we realize the spiritual possibilities with which we are indued by omnipotent Mind, we are lifted up, and all the faculties that we have "called" are lifted up with us. "I, if I be raised on high from the earth, will draw all to myself" (Diaglott).

Wisdom, justice, judgment, are grouped under one head in spiritual consciousness. Webster says in effect that the ground of reason in judgment, which makes conclusions *knowledge,* is found in the connecting link that binds the conceptions together. In religion there is the postulate of a judgment through direct perception of the divine law.

Solomon (Sol-o-mon), the sun man, or solar plexus man, when asked by the Lord what He should give him, chose wisdom above riches and honor; then all the other things were added. Solomon was also a great judge. He had a rare intuition, and he used it freely in arriving at his judgments. He did not rest his investigations on mere facts, but sought out the inner motives. In the case of the two women who claimed the same infant, he commanded an attendant to bring a sword and cut the child in twain and give a half to each woman. Of course the real mother begged him not to do this, and he knew at once that she was the mother.

The appeal of the affectional nature in man for judgment in its highest is in harmony with divine law. We have thought that we were not safe in trusting our feelings to guide us in important issues. But spiritual discernment shows that the "quick-knowing" power of man has its seat of action in the breast. The breastplates worn by Jewish high priests had twelve stones, representing the twelve great powers of the mind. Ready insight into the divine law was the glory of the high priest. Jesus is called the high priest of God, and every man's name is the name Jesus, written large or small, according to his perception of his Son-of-God nature.

Intuition, judgment, wisdom, justice, discernment, pure knowing, and profound understanding are natural to man. All of these qualities, and many more, belong to every one of us by and through his divine sonship. "I said, Ye are gods, and all of you sons of the Most High!" the Christ proclaims in us all. Paul saw Christ waiting at the door of every soul, when he wrote: "Awake, thou that sleepest, and arise from the dead, and Christ shall shine upon thee."

A quickening of our divine judgment arouses in us the judge of all the world. "The wisdom that is from above is first pure, then peaceable." When we call this righteous judge into action, we may find our standards of right and wrong undergoing rapid changes, but if we hold steadily to the Lord as our supreme guide, we shall be led into all righteousness.

Many persons doubt that there is an infinite law of justice working in all things; let them now take heart and know that this law has not worked in their affairs previously because they have not "called" it into activity in the creative center of the soul. When we call our inner forces into action, the universal

law begins its great work in us, and all the laws
both great and small fall into line and work for us.
We do not make the law; the law *is,* and it was
established for our benefit before the world was
formed. Jesus did not make the law of health when
He healed the multitudes; He simply called it into
expression by getting it recognized by those who had
disregarded its existence. Back of the judge is the
law out of which he reads. This fact is recognized
even by those who are intrusted with the carrying
out of man-made laws. Blackstone says that the
judgment, though pronounced and awarded by the
judges, is not their determination or sentence, but the
determination and sentence of the law. So we who
are carrying forward the fulfillment of the law as
inaugurated by Jesus should be wise in recognizing
that the law in all its fullness already exists right
here, waiting for us to identify ourselves with it and
thus allow it to fulfill its righteousness in us and
in all the world.

"I am the vine, ye are the branches." In this symbol
Jesus illustrated a law universal to organisms. The
vine-building law holds good in man's body. The
center of identity is in the head and its activities
are distributed through the nerves and the nerve
fluids to the various parts of the body. The twelve
disciples of Jesus Christ represent the twelve primal
subcenters in man's organism. A study of man's
mind and body reveals this law.

Even physiologists, who regard the body as a mere
physical organism, find certain aggregations of cells

which they have concluded are for no other purpose than for the distribution of intelligence. To one who studies man as mind, these aggregations of cells are regarded as the avenues through which certain fundamental ideas are manifested. We name these ideas the twelve powers of man, identified in man's consciousness as the twelve disciples of the Christ, having twelve houses, villages, cities, or centers in the body through which they act.

Wisdom includes judgment, discrimination, intuition, and all the departments of mind that come under the head of knowing. The house or throne of this wise judge is at the nerve center called the solar plexus. The natural man refers to it as the pit of the stomach. The presiding intelligence at this center knows what is going on, especially in the domain of consciousness pertaining to the body and its needs. Chemistry is its speciality; it also knows all that pertains to the sensations of soul and body. In its highest phase it makes union with the white light of Spirit functioning in the top brain. At the solar plexus also takes place the union between love and wisdom. The disciple who has charge of this center is called James. Volumes might be written describing the activities by which this disciple builds and preserves man's body. Every bit of food that we take into our stomachs must be intelligently and chemically treated at this center before it can be distributed to the many members waiting for this center's wise judgment to supply them with material to build bone, muscle, nerve, eye, ear, hair, nails—in fact every part of the organism. When we study the body and its manifold functions we see how much depends upon the intelligence and ability of the disciple James, who functions through the solar plexus.

When man begins to follow Jesus in the regeneration he finds that he must co-operate with the work of his disciples or faculties. Heretofore they have been under the natural law; they have been fishers in the natural world. Through his recognition of his relation as the Son of God, man co-operates in the original creative law. He calls his faculties out of their materiality into their spirituality. This process is symbolized by Jesus' calling His disciples.

To call a disciple is mentally to recognize that disciple; it is to identify oneself with the intelligence working at a center—for example, judgment, at the solar plexus. To make this identification, one must realize one's unity with God through Christ, Christ being the Son-of-God idea always existing in man's higher consciousness. This recognition of one's sonship and unity with God is fundamental in all true growth. Christ is the door into the kingdom of God. Jesus once spoke of the kingdom as a sheepfold. If man tries to get into this kingdom except through the door of the Christ, he is a thief and a robber. We can call our twelve powers into spiritual activity only through Christ. If we try to effect this end by any other means, we shall have an abnormal, chaotic, and unlawful soul unfoldment.

Having identified oneself with God through Christ, one should center one's attention at the pit of the stomach and affirm:

The wisdom of the Christ mind here active is through my recognition of Christ identified and unified with God. Wisdom, judgment, discrimination, purity, and power are here now expressing themselves in the beauty of holiness. The justice, righteousness, and peace of the Christ mind now harmonize, wisely direct, and surely establish the kingdom of God in His temple, my body. There are no more warring, contentious thoughts in me, for the peace of God is here established, and the lion and the lamb (courage and innocence), sit on the throne of dominion with wisdom and love.

Chapter V

Regenerating Love

W E CANNOT get a right understanding of the relation that the manifest bears to the unmanifest, until we set clearly before ourselves the character of Original Being. So long as we think of God in terms of personality, just so long shall we fail to understand the relation existing between man and God.

Then let us dismiss the thought that God is a man, or even a man exalted far above human characteristics. So long as the concept of a man-God exists in consciousness, there will be lack of room for the true concept, which is that God is First Cause, the Principle from which flow all manifestations. To understand the complex conditions under which the human family exists, we must analyze Being and its creative processes.

Inherent in the mind of Being are twelve fundamental ideas, which in action appear as primal creative forces. It is possible for man to ally himself with and to use these original forces, and thereby co-operate with the creative law, but in order to do this he must detach himself from the forces and enter into the consciousness of the idea lying back of them.

In Scripture the primal ideas in the mind of Being are called the "sons of God." That the masculine "son" is intended to include both masculine and feminine is borne out by the context, and, in fact, the whole history of the race. Being itself must be masculine and feminine, in order to make man in its image and likeness, "male and female."

Analyzing these divine ideas, or sons of God, we find that they manifest characteristics that we readily identify as masculine or feminine. For example, life is a son of God, while love is a daughter of God. Intelligence is a son of God, and imagination is a daughter of God. The evidence that sex exists in the vegetable and animal worlds is so clear that it is never questioned, but we have not so clearly discerned that ideas are also male and female. The union of the masculine and feminine forces in man is most potent in the affectional nature, and that these forces should endure and never be separated by external causes was laid down as a law by Jesus. He said, as recorded in Mark 10:6-9:

From the beginning of the creation, Male and female made he them. For this cause shall a man leave his father and mother, and shall cleave to his wife; and the two shall become one flesh; so that they are no more two, but one flesh. What therefore God hath joined together, let no man put asunder.

We should clearly understand that each of the various ideas, or sons and daughters of God, has identity and in creation is striving with divine might to bring forth its inherent attributes. It is to these ideas, or sons and daughters, that Being, or Elohim, says: "Let us make man in our image, after our likeness" (Gen. 1:26).

Spiritual man is the sum total of the attributes or perfect ideas of Being, identified and individualized. This man is the "only begotten" of Elohim. Jehovah, or I AM THAT I AM, is the name of this divine man. He was manifest as the higher self of Jesus, and in the Scriptures is called the Christ. Jesus named him the "Father in me"; in the book of Matthew, He called Him "Father" more than forty times. Christ is our Father; through Him, Elohim or Original Being brings forth all human beings. It was Jehovah, or I AM, that formed Adam out of the dust of the ground and breathed into his nostrils the breath of life. Breathing is the symbol of inspiration. Jesus breathed upon His disciples, and said to them: "Receive ye the Holy Spirit."

Three primal forces of Being are manifest in the simplest protoplastic cell. Science says that every atom has substance, life, and intelligence. This corresponds with the symbolical creative process of Jehovah, as described in Genesis 2:7. The "dust of the ground" is substance; "breathed" refers to the impartation of intelligence; and the "living soul" is the quickening life. These three constitute the trinity of the natural world, in which the body of man is cast. When one understands the creative processes to be the working of the various principles of Being in the development of man, many inexplicable situations are cleared up. God cannot bring forth without law and order. To produce a man, there must be a combination of forces that at some stages of soul evolution may seem to work against one another; but when one understands that the great creative Mind brings forth under law, reconciliation and consistency are found where inharmony and contradiction seemed dominant.

Of all the daughters of God, love is undoubtedly the most beautiful, enticing, and fascinating. She is by nature exceedingly timid and modest, but when roused she is bold and fearless in the extreme. Mother love is as strong as life and will make every sacrifice to protect offspring. This wholehearted, self-sacrificing aspect of love indicates a spirit deeper and stronger than the animal or the human, and we are forced to admit that it is divine. For this reason mother love is exalted to first place in our analysis of the great passion. But mothers should take heed lest they incorporate human selfishness into the divine love that is expressed in and through them.

The most popular expression of love in the world is the love between men and women. Here also love is misunderstood, and for that reason she has been forced to act in ways that are unnatural to her. She has also been compelled to do things that are abhorrent to her, yet under the compelling power of man's will she could not do otherwise. Right here is a crying need for a purer judgment of love and her right adjustment in the most sacred relation existing between men and women. Love is from God, and it is given to man in its virgin purity. It is the pure essence of Being that binds together the whole human family. Without love we should lose contact with our mother earth, and, losing that, we should fly off into space and be lost in the star dust of unborn worlds. "Gravity" is mortal man's name for love. By the invisible arms of love we are held tight to earth's prolific bosom, and there we find the sweetest home in all the universe. All love of home is founded on man's innate love for this planet. When John Howard Payne wrote "Home, Sweet Home," he was inspired by mother love to sing of the only abiding place of this race—our dear mother earth.

The original Eden of the human family was planted by God on earth, and it is still here. Its prototype is within the human soul, but we have not entered it, because we have not understood the relation that love bears to the original substance of Being, out of which all things are formed.

It is no great task to tell of the higher aspects of love, but who will champion love submerged in human consciousness and smothered with selfishness? You say: "This is not love, but passion and lust." But we should remember that we have laid down, as a foundation principle, that God is love, and, as there is but one God, there can be but one love. This being true, we must find place in the creative law for every manifestation, regardless of its apparent contradictions of the righteousness of First Cause.

Love is submerged or cast down to sense consciousness between men and women in the marriage relation, and great misery floods the world in consequence. This marriage should be a perpetual feast of love, and so it would be if the laws of love were observed. Courtship is usually the most joyous experience that comes to men and women, because love is kept free from lust.

If the laws of conjugality were better understood, the bliss of courtship would continue throughout all the years of married life and divorces would be unknown. It is a fact well known to psychologists that the majority of estrangements between husbands and wives results from the breaking of sex laws. This sin that ends in feebleness and final disintegration of the physical organism is symbolically pictured in the so-called fall of man, in the early chapters of Genesis. Adam and Eve represent the innocent and uneducated powers of the masculine and feminine in every individual. The serpent symbolizes sensation, which combines with life and substance in all living organisms. The desire for pleasure, and for a seemingly short and easy way to get wisdom, tempts the feminine, and she eats, or appropriates. The masculine also eats. In the "cool of the day" (after the heat of passion has cooled off) they both find that they are naked. They have had pleasure with pleasure as the only object, which is contrary to the law of Being. All things should be done with a purpose, with pleasure as a concomitant only. Pleasure lends zest to all action, but it should never be exalted to the high place in consciousness.

Sex indulgence for mere pleasure is an eating or

appropriating of the pure substance that pervades the whole nervous system, which is appropriately compared to a tree. This excess of pleasure is sooner or later followed by equal reaction, which is destructive, and the body cries out in pain. The pleasure we call "good," and the pain we call "evil." Here, in a nutshell, is an explanation of eating of the tree of the "knowledge of good and evil."

When the seminal substance in the organism is conserved and retained, the nerves are charged with a spiritual energy, which runs like lightning through an organism filled with the virgin substance of the soul. When in the ignorance of sensation men and women deplete their substance, the rose of the cheek and the sparkle of the eye fade away. Then the kiss and the touch that were once so satisfying become cold and lifeless.

In the conservation of this pure substance of life is hidden the secret of body rejuvenation, physical resurrection, and the final perpetuation of the whole organism in its transmuted purity. (John saw Jesus in this state of purity, as described in Revelation 1:12-16.) No man can in his own might attain this exalted estate, but through the love of God, demonstrated by Jesus, it is attainable by every one. "For God so loved the world, that he gave his only begotten Son, that whosoever believeth on him should not perish, but have eternal life."

Regeneration is not possible without love. As through the union of the male and female elements the new body of the infant is brought forth, so through the joining of the creative forces of Spirit by souls attuned in love the new body in Christ is speedily formed. The work can be done through individual effort, and there must always be continuous constructive action between the masculine and feminine faculties of soul and body; but the anointing with the precious love of the divine feminine is necessary to the great demonstration. The woman who anointed the head and feet of Jesus "loved much," and Jesus said that that which she did would be remembered wherever the Gospel should be preached in the whole world. This symbolical representation of pouring into the masculine the pure love of the feminine is a guide for all women. All over the world the submerged love of the feminine is crying for release from the sensual dominance of the masculine. The remedy is: Anoint man's head (will) and his feet (understanding) with the Christ love, and he will be purified and satisfied. Not a word need be spoken to bring about the change. If in quietness and confidence the presence and the power of divine love are affirmed, the law will be fulfilled.

Love submerged in sense still retains the remembrance of her virginity, and repels and resists the onslaughts of lust. Some of the most terrible ills are brought upon the body by the misuse of love. This is not the way of freedom; through a steady and firm holding to the one Presence and one Power will the son of man be lifted up, as Moses lifted up the serpent in the wilderness.

Wisdom and love combined are symbolically described in Scripture as the "Lamb slain from the foundation of the world" (A. V.). But now men and women are studying the laws of Being, and in some degree are striving to observe them in the marriage relation. Instead of submerging love in lust, the children of light retain their virgin purity and go hand in hand toward the dawn of a new order, in which there will be a bringing forth of the multitude of waiting souls in a way which is now hidden, but which will be revealed when love is lifted up.

> Call it not love, for Love to heaven is fled
>   Since sweating Lust on earth usurp'd his name;
> Under whose simple semblance he hath fed
>   Upon fresh beauty, blotting it with blame;
> Which the hot tyrant stains and soon bereaves,
> As caterpillars do the tender leaves.
>
> Love comforteth like sunshine after rain,
>   But Lust's effect is tempest after sun;
> Love's gentle spring doth always fresh remain,
>   Lust's winter comes ere summer half be done;
> Love surfeits not, Lust like a glutton dies;
> Love is all truth, Lust full of forged lies.
>   —*Shakespeare.*

CHAPTER VI

Power—Dominion—Mastery

MAN DOES not exercise the power of his spiritual nature, because he lacks understanding of its character and of his relation to the originating Mind in which he exists. From Divine Mind man inherits power over his thought, over the forces of his soul—in truth, power over all ideas. A quickening from on high must precede man's realization of his innate control of thought and feeling. The baptism of the Holy Spirit is a quickening of the spiritual nature, which is reflected in intellect and in body. When one understands the science of Being, one is prepared to receive this baptism and to utilize it along deeper lines of thought. Jesus had taught His disciples and followers, and they were prepared for the baptism that they received on the day of Pentecost.

"Ye shall receive power, when the Holy Spirit is come upon you." Power is essential to the work that Jesus Christ expects His followers to do in the great field of humanity. The command is: Go to every nation and preach the gospel. Man should apply the power of the word to his individual redemption, and he should speak the redeeming word of Spirit to the multitudinous thought people of his own soul and body.

Among the disciples of Jesus Christ, Philip represents the power faculty of the mind. The word "Philip" means "a lover of horses." In physical activity the horse represents power; the ox, strength. Each of the twelve fundamental faculties of man has an ego that reflects, in a measure, the original man idea in God. In the body consciousness the twelve disciples, as egos, have twelve centers, or thrones, from which they exercise their power. The will expresses its dominion from the head; love, from the breast; and power (the ego or disciple whose character we are analyzing in this writing), from the throat. Power is one branch of the great tree; in Genesis it is named "life." The body of the life tree is the spinal cord, over which the motor system, with branches to every part of the organism, exercises its nervous energy.

The power center in the throat controls all the vibratory energies of the organism. It is the open door between the formless and the formed worlds of vibrations pertaining to the expression of sound. Every word that goes forth receives its specific character from the power faculty. When Jesus said, "The words that I have spoken unto you are spirit, and are life," He meant that through the spoken word He conveyed an inner spiritual quickening quality that would enter the mind of the recipient and awaken the inactive spirit and life. When the voice has united with the life of the soul, it takes on a sweetness and a depth that one feels and remembers; the voice that lacks this union is metallic and super-

62

ficial. Voice culture may give one tone brilliancy, but every great singer has the soul contact. But higher and deeper still is the voice of one who has made union with Spirit and who can say with Jesus: "Heaven and earth shall pass away, but my words shall not pass away."

When we understand this power of the word, we have the key to the perpetuity of sacred writings. According to tradition, all the writings of the Bible were destroyed but they were restored by Esdras, who, "remembered in his heart" and rewrote them. Modern discoveries in the realm of mind in a measure explain this mystical statement. We know now that every word that man utters makes an imprint in the astral ethers, and that, when there is consciousness of God life in the mind of the speaker, all his words become living identities and are perpetuated. Any one who develops sufficient spiritual power may enter this book of life within the cosmic mind and read out of its pages.

The mind and the body of man have the power of transforming energy from one plane of consciousness to another. This is the power and dominion implanted in man from the beginning. According to Scripture, "God said, Let us make man in our image, after our likeness; and they shall have dominion over the fish of the sea, and over the fowl of the heaven, and over the cattle, and over all the earth, and over every creeping thing that creepeth upon the earth" (Gen. 1:26; Lesser translation). Paul corroborates this statement by calling attention to the glory of man's inheritance:

Having the eyes of your heart enlightened, that ye may know what is the hope of his calling, what the riches of the glory of his inheritance in the saints, and what the exceeding greatness of his power to usward who believe, according to that working of the strength of his might which he wrought in Christ, when he raised him from the dead, and made him to sit at his right hand in the heavenly *places,* far above all rule, and authority, and power, and dominion, and every name that is named, not only in this world, but also in that which is to come.

In the kingdom of God within man's consciousness, the power disciple plays an important part in controlling the expression of the many emotions, inspirations, and thoughts of the soul. The voice is the most direct avenue of this expression, when man has dominion over the emotions and feelings from which the original impulse arises. The power of love makes the voice rich, warm, and mellow. Man can set love free in his soul by cultivating a loving attitude toward everybody and everything; he may add strength by silently speaking words of strength to each of the disciples sitting upon the twelve thrones within. Power swings open all the doors of soul and body. When one feels vital and energetic, the voice is strong and vibrant and brilliant. When the soul is sorrowful, the body weakens and the voice betrays its lack by its mournful intonation. Through the vibrations of power in the throat, one can feel the power of unity with the higher self more quickly than in any other way. This reveals that ideas rule the man. Jesus affirmed: "All power is given unto me in heaven [mind] and in earth [body]" (A. V.). When Jesus made this affirmation He undoubtedly realized His innate spiritual dominion, and when He consciously attuned His spiritual identity to soul and body, there was a conscious influx of power, and His hearers said that He "taught them as having authority, and not as the scribes."

In the process of regeneration the consciousness of power ebbs and flows, because the old and the new tides of thought act and react in the conscious and the subconscious realms of mind. However, when a disciple realizes his unity with Omnipotence, he is but little disturbed by the changes that go on in his mind and his body; he knows that his spiritual dominion is established, and that firm conviction expresses itself in firm words. Jesus said: "Heaven and earth shall pass away, but my words shall not pass away." Here is the evidence of spiritual power united with the idea of eternity. This union destroys the thought of years and declining power, and when awakened in those who have believed in age it will transform them and make all things new for them.

Every great vocalist has had inner spiritual power as an abiding conviction. This is strikingly illustrated in the indomitable persistency and power with which the famous singer, Galli-Curci, overcame obstacles. In the early stages of her career she was discouraged by opera critics. They told her that she could never make a success, but she persevered; and so she finally mastered every defect of her voice. This is a wonderful lesson to those who are apparently meeting with discouragements, who are tempted to succumb to circumstances and conditions in body and in environment. Take the words of Paul, "None of these things move me" (A. V.), and make unqualified affirmations of your spiritual supremacy.

Some metaphysical schools warn their students against the development of power, because they fear that it will be used in selfish, ambitious ways. It doubtless is true that the personal ego sometimes lays hold of the power faculty and uses it for selfish aggrandizement; we can readily see how what is called the Devil had origin. To be successful in the use of the power of Being, one must be obedient in exercising all the ideas that make man. If there is an assumption of personal power, Lucifer falls like "lightning from heaven," and the adverse or carnal mind goes to and fro in the earth. The casting out of these demons of personality formed a large part of the work of Jesus, and those who follow Him in the regeneration are confronted with similar states of mind and find it necessary to cast out the great demon selfishness, which claims to have power but is a liar and the father of lies.

No disciple can do any great overcoming work without a certain realization of spiritual power, dominion, mastery. Without power, one easily gives up to temporal laws, soul made and man made. The psychic atmosphere is filled with thoughts that are not in harmony with Divine Mind. These psychic thoughts are legion, and to overcome them one must be on one's guard. Jesus said, "Watch." This means that we should quicken our discernment and our ability to choose between the good and the evil. "And why even of yourselves judge ye not what is right?" This wisdom of Spirit is man's through the all-knowing and all-discerning power of Spirit within him, and he need never fear going wrong if he listens to his divine intuition. "Ye shall know the truth, and the truth shall make you free." But man can never be free until he declares his freedom. Jesus Christ said: "I am from above." It is the prerogative of every man to make this declaration and thereby rise above the psychisms of mortal thought. Then do not fear to develop your power and mastery. They are not to be exercised on other people, but on yourself. "He that ruleth his spirit, [is more powerful] than he that taketh a city." Alexander cried because there were no more worlds to conquer, yet he had not conquered his own appetite, and died a drunkard at the age of thirty-three. Today men are striving to acquire power through money, legislation, and man-made government, and falling short because they have not mastered themselves.

Jesus said, "My kingdom is not of this world," yet He set up a kingdom in the world greater than all other kingdoms. In its beginning His kingdom was a very small affair, and the wise and the mighty laughed to scorn the proclamation that He was a king. Yet He was every inch a king. His people have been slow to follow the laws that He promulgated for His kingdom, but men in every walk

67

of life are beginning to comprehend the vital integrity of His edicts, they are seeing that there can be no permanent peace or even civilization on earth until the Golden Rule, laid down by Him, is adopted by nations in commercial and in all other relationships. Business men are teaching the precept of Jesus, "All things therefore whatsoever ye would that men should do unto you, even so do ye also unto them," as fundamental in commercial success. Everywhere we hear them talking co-operation instead of competition. Commercial seers are discerning the dawn of a new day, in which good service instead of big profits will be the goal. Here we see the coming of the Christ "as a thief in the night." The night of ignorance and destructive competition is being burned out.

It follows that every kind of human industry must be carried forward by a power that recognizes the divine law. Man is the power of God in action. To man is given the highest power in the universe, the conscious power of thought. There is a universal creative force that urges man forward to a recognition of the creative power of his individual thought. This force is elemental, and all its attributes come under the dominion of man. When he co-operates with divine principle, man sits on the throne of his authority and the elemental force is subject to him.

But the power and the authority that are to rule in the kingdom of heaven are dependent on man's authority and his rule in the earth. Jesus said to Peter: "Whatsoever thou shalt bind on earth shall be bound in heaven; and whatsoever thou shalt loose on earth shall be loosed in heaven." If man binds or controls the appetites, passions, and emotions in the body (earth), he establishes ability and power to control the same forces in the realms universal, out of which the heavens are formed. When he attains a freedom in the expression of the qualities inherent in soul and body, he expands in power and can set free the elements universal and restore equilibrium between heaven and earth, or Spirit and matter.

When enough people have attained this power, the "new heaven and . . . new earth" (described in the 21st chapter of Revelation) will appear. It will not be necessary for any one to wait for the full complement of overcomers, the mystical 144,000 who are to rule the new world, but each individual who complies with the overcoming law may enter into power with Jesus. It should not be overlooked by the elect that the Scripture reads: "He that overcometh shall inherit these things." To overcome and sit with Jesus on His throne means that man must overcome as He overcame. Jesus overcame the world, the flesh, and the Devil. To overcome the world one must be proof against all its allurements of riches and honor. To overcome the flesh one must spiritualize the five-sense man until material consciousness is raised to spiritual consciousness in feeling, tasting, seeing, hearing, and smelling. This change will ultimate in man's complete mastery of the body and in its final redemption from death.

The Devil is the personal ego who has in his free-

THE TWELVE POWERS OF MAN

dom formed a state of consciousness peculiarly his own. When man lives wholly in the consciousness that personality has built up, he is ruled by the carnal mind, which is the Adversary, or Satan. In the mystery of the cross is hidden the overcoming of Satan. The crucifixion of Jesus is the symbolical representation of the crossing out (destruction) of the carnal mind (Satan) in the redeemed man's consciousness. Christ was not killed on the cross, neither was the body of Jesus destroyed. The "ghost" that Jesus gave up with His last breath was mortality. It was the personal, mortal consciousness that cried, "My God, my God, why hast thou forsaken me?" (This god should be spelled with a small *g*.) The personal-concept God fails to save its worshiper.

When the I AM identity, which is man, becomes so involved in its personal affairs that it ignores God, I AM lays hold of the body and rules all the bodily functions. When this rule is broken by the power of the Christ or supermind, there is a crucifixion. It may seem that Jesus is being crucified, but this is seeming only. Death comes to the Judas consciousness, which "hath a devil" (A. V.), but the body, being closely connected with this usurping mind, passes through suffering and apparent death. This is no more than appearance, because the higher principle, the Christ, resurrects the body and transmutes it into higher spiritual substance, where it enters into harmony or heaven. The climax of man's power and dominion is set forth in the resurrection and ascension of the type man, Jesus.

CHAPTER VII

⋙⋘

The Work of the Imagination in Regeneration

WHEN THE faculties of the mind are understood in their threefold relation—spirit, soul, body—it will be found that every form and shape originated in the imagination. It is through the imagination that the formless takes form. It is well known that the artist sees in mind every picture that he puts on canvas. Man and the universe are a series of pictures in the mind of Being. God made man in His image and likeness. Man, in his turn, is continually making and sending forth into his mind, his body, and the world about him living thought forms embodied and indued with his whole character. These images are formed in the front brain, and clothed with substance and life drawn from subcenters in the body.

Very intellectual people, concentrating the intensity of their thought in the head, fail to connect with the substance, life, and love centers in the body, and their work, although it may be very brilliant, lacks what we term "soul." The thought creations of this type seldom live long. Where the thought form and its substance are evenly balanced, the projected idea endures indefinitely. Jesus was a man thoroughly conversant with this law, and every idea that He clothed has lived and grown in wisdom and power in the minds of those who make union with Him in faith and spiritual understanding. He said: "Heaven and earth shall pass away: but my words shall not pass away."

Among the disciples, Bartholomew represents the imagination. He is called Nathanael in the 1st chapter of John, where it is recorded that Jesus saw him under the fig tree—the inference being that Jesus discerned Nathanael's presence before the latter came into visibility. This would indicate that images of people and things are projected into the imaging chamber of the mind and that by giving them attention one can understand their relation to outer things. Mind readers, clairvoyants, and dreamers have developed this capacity in varying degree. Where consciousness is primary in soul unfoldment there is confusion, because of lack of understanding of the fundamental law of mind action. Forms are always manifestations of ideas. One who understands this can interpret the symbols shown to him in dreams and visions, but lack of understanding of this law makes one a psychic without power. Joseph was an interpreter because he sought the one creative Mind for guidance. "And Joseph answered Pharaoh, saying, It is not in me: God will give Pharaoh an answer of peace." When Pharaoh told him the dream about the fat kine and the lean kine, Joseph at once gave the real meaning of the dream; he understood the metaphysical law. The early Christians had understanding of this law. The same law is in existence today and can be used more effectually by us, the reincarnated followers of Jesus, because mind and its modes of action are now better understood.

The Spirit of truth projects into the chamber of imagery pictures that, rightly understood, will be a sure guide for all people who believe in the omnipresence of mind. Everybody dreams, but the great majority do not attempt to interpret the handwriting on the wall of the mind, or they take their dreams literally and, because the dreams do not come true, consider them foolish. Through ignorance of the law with which imagination works, man has made imagination a byword. We look upon imaginary things as trivial, yet we know that through the imagination we can produce wonderful changes in the body. Studying this law, we find that the character of both soul and body is determined by the imagination and its associated faculties. Paul referred to this power of the imagination when he wrote:

But we all, with unveiled face beholding as in a mirror the glory of the Lord, are transformed into the same image from glory to glory, even as from the Lord the Spirit.

There has been much speculation about the method that Jesus used to impart spiritual understanding to His disciples and other early Christians, who were wonderfully illumined. It is true that the twelve disciples had His personal instruction, but it was apparently preparatory only; the thorough training was to follow. Jesus promised that the Spirit of truth would, in His name, come as teacher, guide, and instructor. He did not say how Spirit would guide and teach those who believed in Him; we gain this conclusion from their experiences in the new school of life to which He introduced them.

It is possible to impart Truth through direct inspiration, but this requires a student with a development of mind superior to the average, and Jesus sought converts in every walk of life. So we find that the simple and universally intelligible avenue of visions and dreams, the work of the imagination, was adopted as an important means by which the believers were instructed and called together. In fact, a large part of the work of the early church was carried forward by this means.

Saul was converted by a vision. Jesus appeared to him in person and rebuked him for his persecution of the Christians, told him that He had a work for him to do, and gave him directions as to his future movements.

And as he [Saul] journeyed, it came to pass that he drew nigh unto Damascus: and suddenly there shone round about him a light out of heaven: and he fell upon the earth, and heard a voice saying unto him, Saul, Saul, why persecutest thou me? And he said, Who art thou, Lord? And he *said,* I am Jesus whom thou persecutest: but rise, and enter into the city, and it shall be told thee what thou must do. And the men that journeyed with him stood speechless, hearing the voice, but beholding no man. And Saul arose from the earth; and when his eyes were opened, he saw nothing; and they led him by the hand, and brought him into Damascus. And he was three days without sight, and did neither eat nor drink.

Those who look to the Holy Spirit for guidance find that its instruction is given to all who believe in Christ, and they are often drawn together by direction of the inner voice, or by a dream, or by a vision. Saul, after beholding the blinding light of the spiritual realms, needed to have his sight restored. The brightness, or high potency, of Jesus' glorified presence had confused his intellectual consciousness, and this had brought about blindness. He needed the harmonious, peace-giving power of one who understood the inner life, and this was found in a certain disciple named Ananias. The Lord said to Ananias in a vision:

Arise, and go the street which is called Straight, and inquire in the house of Judas for one named Saul, a man of Tarsus: for behold, he prayeth; and he hath seen a man named Ananias coming in, and laying his hands on him, that he might receive his sight. But Ananias answered, Lord, I have heard from many of this man, how much evil he did to thy saints at Jerusalem: and here he hath authority from the chief priests to bind all that call upon thy name. But the Lord said unto him, Go thy way: for he is a chosen vessel unto me, to bear my name before the Gentiles and kings, and the children of Israel: for I will show him how many things he must suffer for my name's sake. And Ananias departed, and entered into the house; and laying his hands on him said, Brother Saul, the Lord, *even* Jesus, who appeared unto thee in the way which thou camest, hath sent me, that thou mayest receive thy sight, and be filled with the Holy Spirit. And straightway there fell from his eyes as it were scales, and he received his sight; and he arose and was baptized; and he took food and was strengthened.

The Lord's appearing to Saul, with the conversion of the latter, is considered one of the great miracles of the Bible, but the experience of Ananias is seldom mentioned. Yet we are told in this text that the Lord appeared to Ananias and talked to him, just as He had appeared and talked to Saul, and there was apparently no difference in the real character of the incidents, except such be found in the mental attitude of the participants. Saul was antagonistic and full of fight. Ananias was receptive and obedient; he doubtless had received this sort of guidance many times. From the text we readily discern his spiritual harmony. He knew the reputation of Saul and protested against meeting him, but the Lord explained the situation and Ananias obeyed.

Today disciples of Jesus who are obedient and receptive and believe in the presence and the power of the Master and the Holy Spirit, are everywhere receiving visions and dreams. They are being drawn together and are helping one another to recover from the discords and inharmonies of life. Never before in the history of the race has there been so great a need for spiritual instruction as there is now, and this need is being met by Jesus and His aids in a renaissance of early Christianity and of its methods of instruction.

Spirit imparts its ideas through a universal language. Instead of being explained by words and phrases as used in ordinary language, the idea is formed and projected in its original character. This system of transferring intelligence is called symbolism. It is the only universal and correct means of communicating ideas. For example, if one wished to tell about a procession that he had seen, and could mentally picture it so that others could see it, how much more complete the communication than descriptive words! The mind formulates into thought images every idea that arises in it, and then tries to express it in language, which is nearly always inadequate. The French say: "Words are employed to conceal ideas." As the early disciples of Jesus had to learn that the symbol represents the idea rather than the thing, so modern disciples, following the same line of instruction, should not allow the intellect to materialize their dreams and visions; although they may be puzzled, like Peter, subsequent events will bring to them a clearer understanding of the lesson.

In the 10th chapter of Acts, we read:

Peter went up upon the housetop to pray, about the sixth hour: and he became hungry, and desired to eat: but while they made ready, he fell into a trance; and he beholdeth the heaven opened, and a certain vessel descending, as it were a great sheet, let down by four corners upon the earth: wherein were all manner of four-footed beasts and creeping things of the earth and birds of the heaven. And there came a voice to him, Rise, Peter;

77

kill and eat. But Peter said, Not so, Lord; for I have never eaten anything that is common and unclean. And a voice *came* unto him again the second time, What God hath cleansed, make not thou common. And this was done thrice: and straightway the vessel was received up into heaven.

Now while Peter was much perplexed in himself what the vision which he had seen might mean, behold, the men that were sent by Cornelius, having made inquiry for Simon's house, stood before the gate, and called and asked whether Simon, who was surnamed Peter, were lodging there. And while Peter thought on the vision, the Spirit said unto him, Behold, three men seek thee.

Peter was still bound by the Jewish teaching that there was no salvation for any except those of his faith, and this vision was to break the bondage of such narrowness and show him that the gospel of Jesus Christ is for all people. In a vision the Lord had already instructed Cornelius, the Roman soldier, that he should send certain of his servants to Joppa and fetch Peter to Caesarea.

Some advocates of flesh eating make the mistake of giving a literal interpretation to Peter's vision, holding that the Lord commanded him to kill and eat "all manner of fourfooted beasts and creeping things of the earth and birds of the heaven," and that God has cleansed them and thus prepared them for food for man. If this view of the vision should be carried out literally, we should eat all four-footed animals, including skunks, all the creeping things, and all birds of the air, including vultures. We know, however, that the vision is to be taken in its symbolical meaning. Peter was to appropriate and harmonize in his inner consciousness all thoughts of separation, all uncleanliness and impurity, narrowness, selfishness—the thoughts that bring diversity and separation.

We have within us, bound in the cage of the subconsciousness, all the propensities and the savagery of the animals. In the regeneration these are brought forth and a great reconciliation takes place. We find that there is really nothing unclean, except to human consciousness. In the original creative idealism of Divine Mind, everything was made perfect and sanctified and pronounced "very good." But God did not tell man to eat everything because it was good in its place.

And God said, Behold, I have given you every herb yielding seed, which is upon the face of all the earth, and every tree, in which is the fruit of a tree yielding seed; to you it shall be for food.

When man has regenerated and lifted up the beasts of the field, he will carry out the injunction given to the original Adam and name them "good."

Man's body represents the sum total of the animal world, because in its evolution it has had experience in nearly every type of elemental form. These memories are part of the soul, and in the unregenerate they come to the surface sporadically. Sometimes whole nations seem to revert from culture to savagery without apparent cause, but there is always a cause. These reversions are the result of some violent wrenching of the soul, or of concentration, to the exclusion of everything else, upon a line of thought out of harmony with divine law. When the soul is ripe for its next step in the upward way, a great change takes place, known as regeneration. Jesus referred to this when He said to Nicodemus: "Ye must be born anew." In one of its phases the new birth is a resurrection. All that the soul has passed through has left its image in the subconsciousness, wrought in mind and matter. These images are set free in the regeneration, and man sees them as part of himself. In his "Journal," George Fox, the spiritual-minded Quaker, says:

I was under great temptations sometimes, and my inward sufferings were heavy; but I could find none to open my condition to but the Lord alone, unto whom I cried night and day. I went back into Nottinghamshire, where the Lord shewed me that the natures of those things which were hurtful without, were within the hearts and minds of wicked men. The natures of dogs, swine, vipers, of Sodom and Egypt, Pharaoh, Cain, Ishmael, Esau, etc. The natures of these I saw within, though people had been looking without. I cried to the Lord, saying, "Why should I be thus, seeing I was never addicted to commit those evils?" And the Lord answered, "It was needful I should have a sense of all conditions, how else should I speak of all conditions?" In this I saw the infinite love of God. I saw also, that there was an ocean of darkness and death; but an infinite ocean of light and love, which flowed over the ocean of darkness. In that also I saw the infinite love of God, and I had great openings. As I was walking by the steeple-house side in the town of Mansfield, the Lord said unto me, "That which people trample upon must be thy food." And as the Lord spake he opened to me that people and professors trampled upon the life, even the life of Christ was trampled upon; they fed upon words, and fed one another with words; but trampled under foot the blood of the son of God, which blood was my life: and they lived in their airy notions talking of him. It seemed strange to me at the first, that I should feed on that which the high professors trampled upon; but the Lord opened it clearly to me by his eternal Spirit and power.

In the regeneration man finds that he has, in the part of his soul called the natural man, animal propensities corresponding to the animals in the outer world. In the pictures of the mind, these take form as lions, horses, oxen, dogs, cats, snakes, and the birds of the air. The visions of Joseph, Daniel, John, and other Bible seers were of this character. When man understands that these animals represent thoughts, working in the subconsciousness, he has a key to the many causes of bodily conditions. It is clear to him that the prophets of old were using symbols to express ideas, and he sees that to interpret these symbols he must learn what each represents, in order to get the original meaning.

According to Genesis, the original creation was ideal, and through man the ideal was given character and form. Adam gave character to all the beasts of the field: "and whatever the man called every living creature, that was the name thereof." To the spiritually wise it is revealed that, when man is fully redeemed, he redeems and purifies and uplifts the animals in himself. The animal world will go through a complete transformation when the race is

81

redeemed. As Isaiah says, "the wolf and the lamb shall feed together, and the lion shall eat straw like the ox." Some even go further than this, and say that in the millennium there will be no necessity for animals; that they are, in reality, the dissipated forces of the human family and that when those forces are finally gathered into the original fount in the subjective, there will be no more animals in the objective; that in this way man will be immensely strengthened and a certain connection will be made between the so-called material and the spiritual.

CHAPTER VIII

❦

Understanding

REFERENCE to the dictionary shows the words wisdom, understanding, knowledge, and intelligence to be so closely related that their definitions overlap in a most confusing way. The words differ in meaning, but various writers on the mind and its faculties have given definitions of these words in terms that directly oppose the definitions of other writers. There are two schools of writers on metaphysical subjects, and their definitions are likely to confuse a student unless he knows to which class the writer belongs. First are those who handle the mind and its faculties from an intellectual standpoint, among whom may be mentioned Kant, Hegel, Mill, Schopenhauer, and Sir William Hamilton. The other school includes all the great company of religious authors who have discerned that Spirit and soul are the causing factors of the mind. Compilers of dictionaries have consulted the former class for their definitions, and we have in consequence an inadequate set of terms to express the deep things of the mind. Even Christian metaphysicians who belong in the second classification have no clear understanding of the two great realms of mind: first, that in which pure ideas and pure logic rule; and second, the realm in which the thoughts and the actions of the mind are concerned with reason and the relation of ideas in the outer world. It is only in the last half century that large numbers of Christians have discerned that Jesus taught a metaphysical science.

Poets are natural mystics and metaphysicians, and in their writings we find the safest definitions of the names used to represent the actions of the mind. Poets nearly always make the proper distinction between wisdom and understanding. Tennyson says, "Knowledge comes, but wisdom lingers." Spiritual discernment always places wisdom above the other faculties of mind and reveals that knowledge and intelligence are auxiliary to understanding. Intellectual understanding comes first in the soul's development, then a deeper understanding of principles follows, until the whole man ripens into wisdom.

> 'Tis the sunset of life gives me mystical lore,
> And coming events cast their shadows before.

The writings of the Hebrew prophets are good examples of original inspiration, which is wisdom. Solomon was famous for his wisdom. Jehovah appeared to him in a dream and said: "Ask what I shall give thee." Solomon replied: "Give thy servant therefore an understanding heart to judge thy people, that I may discern between good and evil." Pleased because Solomon had asked for wisdom instead of riches and honor, the Lord said:

Behold, I have done according to thy word; lo I have given thee a wise and an understanding heart . . . And I have also given thee that which thou hast not asked, both riches and honor . . . And Solomon awoke; and, behold, it was a dream.

It was after this occurrence that two women appealed to Solomon to decide which of them really was the mother of the child that they both claimed.

And the king said, Fetch me a sword. . . . And the king said, Divide the living child in two, and give half to the one, and half to the other. Then spake the woman whose the living child was unto the king, for her heart yearned over her son, and she said, Oh, my lord, give her the living child, and in no wise slay it. But the other said, It shall be neither mine nor thine; divide it. Then the king answered and said, Give her the living child, and in no wise slay it: she is the mother thereof. And all Israel heard of the judgment which the king had judged; and they feared the king: for they saw that the wisdom of God was in him, to do justice.

The foregoing is a fine example of intuitive knowing. Instead of indulging in the usual taking of testimony and the various methods of proving the case by witnesses, Solomon appealed directly to the heart and got the truth quickly. No amount of exoteric testimony would have accomplished what the appeal to love brought forth at once.

Although it is sometimes difficult to determine between pure knowing and the quick perception of the intellect, the decision can always be made truly, based upon the presence of the affectional nature.

Great philosophers in every age have testified to the activity of a supermind quality, which they have variously named. Socrates had it. He called it his *daemon*. Plato named it *pure reason*. Jesus called it the kingdom of the heavens.

In an article by M. K. Wisehart, printed in the American Magazine for June, 1930, entitled "A Close Look at the World's Greatest Thinker," Professor Albert Einstein is quoted as saying:

" 'Every man knows that in his work he does best and accomplishes most when he has attained a proficiency that enables him to work intuitively. That is, there are things which we come to know so well that we do not know how we know them. So it seems to me in matters of principle. Perhaps we live best and do things best when we are not too conscious of how and why we do them.'

"He spoke of the great extent to which intuition figures in his work, and gave me to understand that the ability to work by intuition is one that can be acquired in any walk of life. It comes as the result of prolonged effort and reflection and application and failures and trying again. Then, in the end, one knows things without knowing how one knows them! And I gathered that the Professor meant to say that no man knows anything until he knows it in this thorough, instinctive way.

"People frequently ask Professor Einstein whether, as a scientist, he believes in God. Usually he answers: 'I do not believe in a God who maliciously or arbitrarily interferes in the personal affairs of mankind. My religion consists of an humble admiration for the vast power which manifests itself in that small part of the universe which our poor, weak minds can grasp!'

"In a discussion, when the Professor is impressed by the correctness of his own views or those of another, he will suddenly exclaim: 'Yes! So it is! It is just! It must be so! I am quite sure that God could not have made it different!' For him, God is as valid as a scientific argument.

"At one time, after prolonged concentration upon a single problem (it lasted for nearly four years), the Professor suffered a complete physical collapse. With it came severe stomach trouble. A celebrated specialist said: 'You must not get out of bed! You cannot stand on your feet for a long time to come.'

" 'Is this the will of God?' queried the Professor instantly. 'I think not! The voice of God is from within us. Something within me tells me that every day I must get up at least once. I must go to the piano and play! The rest of the day I will spend in bed! This I am prepared to accept as the will of God!'

"And with the will of God, as set forth by Einstein, the specialist had to be content. Every day the Professor got up, put his bathrobe over his nightshirt, and went to the piano to play.

"I asked many questions to elicit the lessons of his experience that might be of most use to the rest of us. I learned that he reads little. 'Much reading after a certain age,' he says, 'diverts the mind from its creative pursuits. Any man who reads too much and uses his own brain too little falls into lazy habits of thinking, just as the man who spends too much time in the theaters is apt to be content with living vicariously instead of living his own life.

" 'I have only two rules which I regard as principles of conduct. The first is: Have no rules. The second is: Be independent of the opinion of others.' "

So we find that there is in man a knowing capacity transcending intellectual knowledge. Nearly every one has at some time touched this hidden wisdom and has been more or less astonished at its revelations. It certainly is a most startling experience to find ourselves giving forth logical thoughts and words without preparation or forethought, because we nearly always arrive at our conclusions through a process of reasoning. However, the reasoning process is often so swift that we are likely to think that it is true inspiration, especially when we have received either the reflected uplift of other wise ones or the baptism of the Holy Spirit. This quickening of the intellect is the John-the-Baptist or intellectual illumination that precedes the awakening of the ideal, the Christ understanding. Some Truth students become so enamored of the revelations that they receive through the head that they fail to go on to the unfoldment of the One who baptizes in "Holy Spirit and in fire." The Old Testament writers had a certain understanding of the first and the second opening of the mind to spiritual truth; Isaiah said:

The voice of one that crieth, Prepare ye in the wilderness the way of Jehovah; make level in the desert a high way for our God.

Elijah had intellectual illumination, and the Israelites were taught that he would come again as a forerunner of the Messiah. Jesus said that Elijah had come again in the personality of John the Baptist:

> I say unto you, that Elijah is come already, and they knew him not . . . Then understood the disciples that he spake unto them of John the Baptist.

The history of the Israelites is a sort of moving picture of man's soul and body development. When we understand the psychology of the different scenes, we know what we have passed through or will pass through in our journey from sense to soul.

Intellectual understanding of Truth, as given in the first baptism, is a tremendous step in advance of sense consciousness, and its possession brings a temptation to use for selfish ends the wisdom and the power thereby revealed. When Jesus received this baptism He was "led up of the Spirit into the wilderness to be tempted of the devil" (personal ego) before he could take the next degree in Son-of-God consciousness.

But Jesus knew that the illumination of the personal is not the fulfillment of the law, and He rejected every temptation to use His understanding for selfish ends.

Unless the disciple is very meek he will find the mortal ego strongly asserting its arguments for the application of the power of Spirit to personal needs. The god of mammon is bidding high for souls that have received the baptism of Spirit, and many sell out, but their end is dust and ashes. No man can serve two masters; one cannot serve both God and Mammon.

When we discover in ourselves a flow of thought that seems to have been evolved independently of the reasoning process, we are often puzzled about its origin and its safety as a guide. In its beginnings this seemingly strange source of knowledge is often turned aside as a daydream; again it seems a distant voice, an echo of something that we have heard and forgotten. One should give attention to this unusual and usually faint whispering of Spirit in man. It is not of the intellect and it does not originate in the skull. It is the development, in man, of a greater capacity to know himself and to understand the purpose of creation. The Bible gives many examples of the awakening of this brain of the heart, in seers, in lawgivers, and in prophets. It is accredited as coming from the heart. The nature of the process is not explained; one who is in the devotional stage of unfoldment need not know all the complex movements of the mind in order to get the message of the Lord. It is enough to know that the understanding is opened in both head and heart when man gives himself wholly to the Lord.

This relation of head and heart is illustrated in the lives of John the Baptist and Jesus. They were cousins; the understanding of the head bears a close relation to the wisdom of the heart. They both received the baptism of Spirit, John preceding Jesus and baptizing Him. Here the natural order of spiritual illumination is illustrated. Man receives first an intellectual understanding of Truth which he transmits to his heart, where love is awakened. The Lord reveals to him that the faculty of love is the greatest of all the powers of man and that head knowledge must decrease as heart understanding increases.

However, we should remember that none of the faculties is eliminated in the regeneration. Among the disciples of Jesus, Thomas typifies the head, representing reason and intellectual perception. Jesus did not ignore Thomas's demand for physical evidence of His identity, but respected it. He convinced Thomas by corporal evidence that there had been a body resurrection; that He was living, not in a psychical or ghost body, but in the same body that had been crucified.

Jesus plainly taught that He had attained control of the life in the body and could take it up or lay it down. We may construe the death and the resurrection of Jesus in various ways, many of them fanciful and allegorically far removed from practical life, but the fact remains that there is good historical evidence of the physical reality of the Resurrection in its minutest detail.

Spiritual understanding shows us that the resurrection of the body from death is not to be confined to Jesus, but is for all men who comprehend Truth and apply it as Jesus applied it. He had the consciousness of the new flood of life that comes to all who open their minds and their bodies to the living

Word of God, and He knew that it would raise the atomic vibration of His organism above the disintegrating thought currents of the earth and thus would save His flesh from corruption.

When Jesus told the Jews what He discerned, they said that He was crazy ("hath a demon"). One who teaches and practices the higher understanding and reality of man's relation to the creative law is not sane—from the viewpoint of mortal man.

When the higher understanding in Jesus proclaimed, "Verily, verily, I say unto you, If a man keep my word, he shall never see death," they took up stones to cast at Him. This startling claim of the power of the word of Truth to save one from death is beyond all human reason, and it is resented by the material thoughts, which are as hard as rocks.

Jesus did not let the limited race thought about man keep Him from doing the works of Spirit. He knew that the light of Truth had arisen in His consciousness and He was not afraid to affirm it. He went right ahead healing the sick and teaching the Truth as He saw it, regardless of the traditions of the Hebrew fathers, Abraham, Isaac, and Jacob. He kept the light shining in His consciousness by being loyal to it and by making for Himself the highest statements of Truth that He could conceive. The Christ mind speaking in Him said: "I am the light of the world."

Spiritual understanding is developed in a multitude of ways; no two persons have exactly the same experience. One may be a Saul, to whom the light comes in a blinding flash, while to another the light may come gently and harmoniously. The sudden breaking forth of the light indicates the existence of stored-up reservoirs of spiritual experience, gained from previous lives. Jesus saw that Saul had a spiritual capacity that, turned into right channels, would do great good; so He took some pains to awaken in Saul the true light and thereby restrain the destructive zeal that possessed him. "He is a chosen vessel unto me, to bear my name before the Gentiles and kings, and the children of Israel."

The spiritual nature develops in man as the other attributes of his character develop. "As he thinketh within himself, so is he" is a statement of the law that has no exceptions. Man develops the capacity to do that which he sets out to do. If one makes no start one never goes.

> In idle wishes fools supinely stay;
> Be there a will, then wisdom finds a way.

No one ever attained spiritual consciousness without striving for it. The first step is to ask. "Ask, and it shall be given you; seek, and ye shall find; knock, and it shall be opened unto you." Prayer is one form of asking, seeking, and knocking. Then make your mind receptive to the higher understanding, through silent meditations and affirmations of Truth. The earnest desire to understand spiritual things will open the way and revelations within and without will follow. In Daniel 10:12 it is writtten:

93

Fear not, Daniel; for from the first day that thou didst set thy heart to understand, and to humble thyself before thy God, thy words were heard: and I am come for thy words' sake.

Daniel humbled himself in the presence of the universal Mind, and thereby opened his understanding and made himself receptive to the cosmic consciousness. Daniel and his companions were superior in wisdom and understanding to all the native magicians and seers in the whole Babylonian realm. The Scriptures say that God gave Daniel knowledge and skill in all learning and wisdom, and "Daniel had understanding in all visions and dreams." Cultivate purity of mind and body, and you will open the way for the higher thoughts, as did Daniel. He "purposed in his heart that he would not defile himself with the king's dainties, nor with the wine which he drank: therefore he requested of the prince of the eunuchs that he might not defile himself."

Spiritual understanding is developed in the feminine realm of the soul. This development is pictured in Acts 16:14: "And a certain woman named Lydia, a seller of purple, of the city of Thyatira, one that worshipped God, heard us: whose heart the Lord opened."

Thyatira means "burning incense"; it represents the intense desire of the soul for the higher expressions of life. When this inner urge comes forth with power (seller of purple), the Lord opens the heart and we receive the heavenly message, like the disciples who said one to another: "Was not

our heart burning within us, while he spake to us
in the way, while he opened to us the scriptures?"

Wisdom consisteth not in knowing many things, nor
even in knowing them thoroughly; but in choosing and in
following what conduces the most certainly to our lasting
happiness and true glory.—*Landor.*

Knowledge dwells in heads replete with thoughts of
other men, wisdom in minds attentive to their own.
—*Cowper.*

She [knowledge] is earthly of the mind, but wisdom
heavenly of the soul.—*Tennyson.*

> Create in me a clean heart, O God;
> And renew a right spirit within me.
> —*Psalms 51:10.*

> For wisdom shall enter into thy heart,
> And knowledge shall be pleasant unto thy soul.
> —*Proverbs 2:10.*

> But the path of the righteous is as the dawning light.
> That shineth more and more unto the perfect day.
> —*Proverbs 4:18.*

> A tranquil heart is the life of the flesh;
> But envy is the rottenness of the bones.
> —*Proverbs 14:30.*

> My son, forget not my law;
> But let thy heart keep my commandments.
> —*Proverbs 3:1.*

> Trust in Jehovah with all thy heart,
> And lean not upon thine own understanding:
> In all thy ways acknowledge him,
> And he will direct thy paths.
> —*Proverbs 3:5, 6.*

Happy is the man that findeth wisdom,
And the man that getteth understanding.
For the gaining of it is better than the gaining of silver,
And the profit thereof than fine gold.
She is more precious than rubies:
And none of the things thou canst desire are to be com-
    pared unto her.
Length of days is in her right hand;
In her left hand are riches and honor.
Her ways are ways of pleasantness,
And all her paths are peace.
She is a tree of life to them that lay hold upon her:
And happy is every one that retaineth her.
Jehovah by wisdom founded the earth;
By understanding he established the heavens.

—Proverbs 3:13-19.

CHAPTER IX

The Will Is the Man

OUR CAPTION is quoted from an ancient meta-physical teaching, the origin of which is lost in antiquity. The idea is that the development of the will is possible only through the development of the mind as a whole, and as man is mind, "the will is the man." This conclusion is reached because the will moves to action all the other faculties of the mind and seems to be the whole process.

However, a careful analysis of the various factors entering into an action reveals other equally important attributes of man, and we cannot wholly admit that "the will is the man." The will is undoubtedly the focal point around which all action centers, when there is harmony of mind; but the rule has been accepted by schools of philosophy from most ancient times down to the present that the will and the understanding are very closely related —the understanding comprehending all our speculative, the will all our active, powers. This close relationship is symbolically taught in the Bible, and it appeals to man's reason and is confirmed by his observation.

Jacob, representing the I AM (I will be what I will to be), had twelve sons, one of whom was Joseph, "the dreamer." Joseph represents the imagination, by which all forms and shapes are brought into manifestation. In the development of the soul, certain faculties are given prominence. After they run their race, other faculties that have been held in reserve come forward. When the period of rest comes, the Scriptures recite that a certain one "died, old and full of days." As man goes forward in his unfoldment, there is sometimes a tendency toward the surface of consciousness, or the phenomenal, and a gradual loss of interest in the original sources of action. The phenomenal phase of creation is so interesting that the soul sometimes becomes bewildered in its study or its pleasure, and the originating cause may be ignored to the point of forgetfulness. This cessation of creative activity by the imagination (Joseph) is described in these words: "So Joseph died, being a hundred and ten years old: and they embalmed him, and he was put in a coffin in Egypt." This means metaphysically that when the imagination in a life span has fulfilled its mission as a creative power it falls asleep, but it is preserved in the realms of darkness (Egypt).

Joseph's number is eleven. He was the eleventh son, and his age when he stopped active work and fell asleep (110) represents the completeness of the dispensation of that faculty's activity; the cipher indicates an endless capacity for expression. The figure given as the age of a Biblical character usually represents the subject's place in his evolution. Joseph completed his evolution to the eleventh degree plus. The cipher means that he has more to demonstrate.

Jesus' number is twelve. He was wise at the age of twelve.

Adam was third in the Godhead (God, Christ, man). He lived 930 years, according to scriptural chronology. This number tells us that he is third in the trinity, has the capacity of the twelvefold man, but has unfolded only three of the twelve faculties. The order of the numbers indicates the harmony of his unfoldment. In this instance it was orderly—the naught denotes future progress uninterrupted.

Seth, the son whom Adam begat "in his own likeness, after his image," represents the awakening of spiritual consciousness. "Then began men to call upon the name of Jehovah." Seth's years were 912. Here the trinity and the twelvefold man are epitomized, and we see that Seth was the birth, in Adam, of Adam's own original character, even the image and likeness of Elohim. In the figure nine the trinity is repeated three times, once for each of its identities, God, Christ, man; then the twelve powers of man are added. Again the total of the digits is twelve, the number of divine man demonstrated.

We have called attention to the metaphysical meaning of the chronology of these Biblical characters in order to illustrate more fully the manner in which the faculties are developed. It will be seen that in man is implanted the likeness of God, which man develops in a long series of personalities. The process of forming a soul may be compared to the development, in a photographic negative, of the image that has been imprinted upon the sensitive plate but cannot be seen until it has been put through a regular developing process. When Adam had a spiritual awakening he perceived the truth of his identity in God, and thereby begat Seth, the original image and likeness of spiritual man, imprinted upon him by the Word of creative mind. Then the worship of Jehovah was restored in man's whole consciousness, for a time at least.

Coming down the chronological stream, we find that Joseph's place was taken by two sons. "And Joseph called the name of the first-born Manasseh: For, *said he,* God hath made me forget all my toil, and all my father's house. And the name of the second called he Ephraim: For God hath made me fruitful in the land of my affliction." The mother of these sons was Asenath, daughter of Potiphera, Egyptian priest of On. Asenath means "peril." She represents the feminine or love side of the natural man. From this intricate symbology we discern that two faculties of the mind were given birth. The eldest son, Manasseh, had power to forget, to erase by denial, through an understanding of Truth, all the accumulated burden of thoughts, even to that of heredity, "all my father's house." The other son, Ephraim, could add to by affirmation and make fruitful the land that seemed to be a place of affliction. These two sons of Joseph inherited his allotment in the Promised Land, which symbolizes the perfected body. The front brain is the field of operation for these closely related faculties—imagination, understanding, and will. When man's will is working strongly he corrugates his brow, and his quick understanding causes his eyes to flash.

When the imagination is subjective and spiritual and the will and the understanding are objective and alert, we have the creative artist. Then the understanding develops its greatest freedom and originality. It is no longer bound by the traditions of the past in literature, art, music, drama, science, or religion, but launches out into the deep and brings up the "pearl of great price," original creative genius and life. Then the energetic will makes fruitful by its activity all the inspirations of the awakened man.

These two closely related forces of the mind are dominant in the race because their practicality is necessary in the soul's free development. If the imagination were wholly in command, it would eventually run into a riot of daydreams or fanciful schemes that could not be worked out successfully in a world where natural law is inexorable. It is this "peril" (Asenath) that the mind considers, and brings forth, in sequence, will and understanding. "The highest and most excellent thing in man," says Goethe, "is formless, and we must guard against giving it shape in anything save noble deeds."

Man is a free agent in the possession and the use of the faculty of will. Freedom of will has been variously regarded and defined. It is the subject of volumes of theological literature and also the rock on which religionists have split. The theory of predestination relieves man of all responsibility. If man's existence and every act is fixed by God, then there can be no mental or moral freedom. If man cannot determine the character of his acts, he has neither understanding nor will, hence he is a mere puppet.

The understanding and the will should be especially active in one who would master the sensations of the body. Potiphar's wife represents the sense consciousness of the soul which tempts us to meet its desires, and, when we deny it, has us imprisoned. This means that when a certain habit in the sense consciousness is refused expression, it reacts and for a time seems to prevent our expressing even the good. But let us patiently bide our time; the higher will will yet show its God-given power.

The several visits of Joseph's brothers to Egypt for corn, and the final reconciliation, are symbolical representations of the manner in which we make connection with the obscured vitality within the organism and finally bring all our faculties into conjunction with it.

Volumes might be written with Joseph as a text. In his history, as given in Genesis, some of the most interesting processes of regeneration are symbolized. This hidden realm within the subconsciousness is in an Egyptian, or obscured, state to most of us. Yet it is a great kingdom, and its king is Pharaoh, ruler of the sun, or the "brain" and nerve center, which physiology names the solar plexus. This is the brain of the physical man, and it directs the circulation, digestion, assimilation, and so forth. Students of mind have discovered that the solar plexus is the organ through which a ruling thought in the head is carried into the body. He of the "hard heart," who would not let the people go, is human will, acting through the solar plexus, or city of the sun.

The spiritual life in the subconsciousness (Children of Israel in Egypt) is often prevented from expressing itself by the opposition of the will. If the understanding decides that what it conceives to be the natural law shall be the limit of expression, there is further bondage and there are harder tasks. Any hard, dictatorial, or willful state of mind will harden the heart. This state of mind acts through the solar plexus (the distributing station for building forces of the body), and thereby brings its limitations upon the whole system. Hardened arteries are the result of hard thoughts, this hardness originates in the will. Jehovah represents the law of the I AM in action.

The ambiguity in the term "motive" has caused much of the controversy that has raged over free will. The champions of free will commonly suppose that before performing an act a man is affected by various motives, none of which necessarily determines his act. Their opponents, on the other hand, argue that there is no such thing as this unmotivated choice. Some hold that free will proper consists of choice only as between higher and lower good. Some regard it as consisting in the power to do as one pleases or chooses. Others define it as the power to do or to choose as one should.

According to some academic metaphysicians, the

freedom of the will includes the power to act contrary to all of one's own motives or inclinations or tendencies, this power being inherent in the will. It is readily seen that this thing called "motive" is another name for understanding, and that it is a necessary adjunct to that faculty. But not all people use understanding as the headlight for both motive and will. The undisciplined mind feels the impulse that lies behind motive, and acts without considering either cause or effect. This is partaking of the knowledge of good and evil without heeding the voice of wisdom—the sin of Adam, undeveloped man. Understanding may be illumined by the Christ mind, and thus receive the light that "lighteth every man, coming into the world." Without this light man breaks the law in nearly every act. The divorcement of understanding from will has led to endless controversies between those who have written and debated about the necessity for man's having free will, and those who, because of the evils that have come upon man through ignorant willing, have advocated the utter effacement of the will.

We do not need less will; we need more understanding. Jesus (spiritual light) showed Thomas (intellectual understanding) the wounds that ignorance had inflicted upon the innocent body. Jesus' disciples represented His own faculties of mind. When He called them they were ignorant and undisciplined children of the natural world. But the image and likeness of the creative mind was upon them, to discipline them in the wisdom of the Christ (spiritual I AM).

As the executive power of the mind, human will is the negative pole of spiritual decision. Right here is where those who study man from a personal viewpoint fail in their estimate of his power and his accountability. As mortal, living in a material world, he seems circumscribed and limited in capacity and destiny. Philosophers have studied man in this cage of the mind, and their conclusions have been that he is little better than a reasoning animal.

But there is a higher and truer estimate of man, and that estimate is made from what the academic school of philosophy would call the purely speculative side of existence. Failing to discern his spiritual origin, they fail in estimating his real character. As a product of the natural man, will is often a destructive force. Nearly all our systems of training children have been based upon breaking the will in order to gain authority over the child and obedience from him. We should remember that the right to exercise freedom of will was given to man in the beginning, according to Genesis, and that will should always be given its original power and liberty.

It is possible, however, for man so to identify his consciousness with Divine Mind that he is moved in every thought and act by that Mind. Jesus attained this unity; when He realized that He was willing not in the personal but in the divine, He said: "Not my will, but thine, be done."

Many sincere Christians have tried to follow in the way of Jesus, and they have negatively sub-

mitted their will to God. But they have not attained
the power or the authority of Jesus by so doing.
The reason is that they have not raised their will
to the positive spiritual degree. Jesus was not negative in any of His faculties, and He did not teach
a doctrine of submission. He gave, to those who
went forth preaching the Gospel, the power and
authority of the Holy Spirit. In Mark 16:16-18 it is
recorded that Jesus says: "He that believeth and is
baptized shall be saved; but he that disbelieveth
shall be condemned. And these signs shall accompany them that believe: in my name shall they cast
out demons; they shall speak with new tongues;
they shall take up serpents, and if they drink any
deadly thing, it shall in no wise hurt them; they shall
lay hands on the sick, and they shall recover." We
must believe in the higher powers and be immersed
in the omnipresent water of life. If we fail to exercise faith in things spiritual, we are condemned to
the prison of materiality.

Some Christians believe that God's will toward
men varies, that His will changes, that He chastises
the disobedient and punishes the wicked. This view
of God's character is gained from the Old Testament. Jehovah was the tribal God of the Israelites
as Baal was of the Philistines. Men's concepts of
God are measured by their spiritual understanding.
The Jehovah, of Moses, is quite different from the
Father, of Jesus, yet they are spiritually one and
the same. "It is not the will of your Father who is
in heaven, that one of these little ones should per-

ish," is the teaching of Jesus. He bore witness that the will of God is that men should not suffer—that through Him they should have complete escape from sin, sickness, and even death. "God so loved the world, that he gave his only begotten Son, that whosoever believeth on him should not perish, but have eternal life." The sin, sickness, suffering, and death that men experience are not punishment willed by God; they are results of broken law. The law is good; men have joy, satisfaction, and life in everlasting harmony, when they keep the law. Creation would not be possible without rules governing the created.

It is error for any one to submit his will to the control of any personality. The personal exercise of will by personal understanding is short-sighted and selfish; hence it is never safe to allow oneself to be led by the direction or advice of another. Practice the presence of God until you open your consciousness to the inflow of the omnipresent, all-knowing mind, then affirm your unity with that mind until you know and fully realize, through the many avenues of wisdom, just what you should do. This acquirement of a knowledge of the divine will is not the work of an instant; it results from patient and persistent spiritual study, prayer, and meditation. Even Jesus, with His exalted understanding, found it necessary to pray all night. All who have found the peace and the power of God have testified to the necessity of using prayer in the soul's victory.

One should not intellectually will to bring about

results for oneself or for another. The difference between the personal will and the universal will can be known by one who practices thought control in the silence.

Affirmations made in the head alone are followed by a feeling of tension, as if bands were drawn across the forehead. When this state of mind sinks back into the subconsciousness, the nerves become tense; if the practice is continued, nervous prostration follows.

Stubborn, willful, resistant states of mind congest the life flow; they are followed by cramps and congestions. The will often compels the use of the various organs of the body beyond their normal capacity, and the results are found in strained nerves and strained muscles and in impaired sight and impaired hearing. Disobedient children have earache, showing the direct result that self-will has on the nerves of the ear. Deaf persons should be treated for freedom from willfulness and obstinacy. In the present state of race consciousness, all people use the intellectual will to excess. The remedy is daily relaxation, meditation, prayer.

Will, as exercised by man, is the negative pole of the great executive force of the universe. The recognition of this in silent meditation opens the will to the inflow of this mighty, moving principle, and the power that moves to action the members of the body reaches into the invisible realm of ideas and controls the elements. It was comprehension of the will universal that enabled Jesus to say to the wind and the waves, "Peace, be still."

Life, liberty, and the pursuit of happiness are the inalienable rights of man, and they should never be interfered with. Hypnotism, mesmerism, and mediumship are based upon the submission of one will to another. The one who desires control demands another's submission in mind and body to his own willed thoughts and words of directive power. The effect upon the one who submits is always weakening, and, if continued, results in a mental negation that makes him the victim of evil influences too numerous to mention.

"Not my will, but thine, be done" is one of the most far-reaching affirmations of Jesus, and those who follow Him and keep His sayings are finding great peace and relaxation of mind and body.

Jesus, the mighty helper, is always present with those who are earnestly seeking to be Christians and to keep the divine law.

CHAPTER X

~~~~~~

Spiritual Law and Order

THE 23d chapter of Matthew is a philippic against ecclesiastical ritualism. Jesus arraigns the scribes and the Pharisees before the bar of the divine law and charges them with a long list of crimes committed in the name of religion. He makes charge after charge of delinquency in spiritual observance of the law and warns His disciples and the multitudes to beware of the works of these blind leaders of the blind. Among other accusations He says:

Yea, they bind heavy burdens and grievous to be borne, and lay them on men's shoulders . . . all their works they do to be seen of men . . . they . . . love the chief place at feasts, and the chief seats in the synagogues . . . and to be called of men, Rabbi. But be not ye called Rabbi: for one is your teacher, and all ye are brethren. And call no man your father on the earth: for one is your Father, *even* he who is in heaven. Neither be ye called masters: for one is your master, *even* the Christ. But he that is greatest among you shall be your servant. And whosoever shall exalt himself shall be humbled; and whosoever shall humble himself shall be exalted.

But woe unto you, scribes and Pharisees, hypocrites! because ye shut the kingdom of heaven against men: for ye enter not in yourselves, neither suffer ye them that are entering in to enter.

Woe unto you, scribes and Pharisees, hypocrites! for ye

compass sea and land to make one proselyte; and when he is become so, ye make him twofold more a son of hell than yourselves. . . .

Woe unto you, scribes and Pharisees, hypocrites! for ye tithe mint and anise and cummin, and have left undone the weightier matters of the law, justice, and mercy, and faith: but these ye ought to have done, and not to have left the other undone. Ye blind guides, that strain out the gnat, and swallow the camel!

Woe unto you, scribes and Pharisees, hypocrites! for ye cleanse the outside of the cup and of the platter, but within they are full from extortion and excess. Thou blind Pharisee, cleanse first the inside of the cup and of the platter, that the outside thereof may become clean also. . . .

Woe unto you, scribes and Pharisees, hypocrites! for ye build the sepulchres of the prophets, and garnish the tombs of the righteous, and say, If we had been in the days of our fathers, we should not have been partakers with them in the blood of the prophets.

All these "woes" are to those who are living in the letter instead of in the spirit of the law. But Jesus did not condemn religion, nor religious organizations. His denunciations were aimed at those who profess to teach and to follow the law but fall short in carrying it out in their lives.

Right here, however, religious teachers should be on their guard in framing tenets for religious organizations. Do not dogmatize in creed, or statement of Being, as a governing rule of thought and action for those who join your organization. These things are limitations, and they often prevent the free development of the soul because of foolish insistence on consistency. The creed that you write

THE TWELVE POWERS OF MAN

today may not fit the viewpoint of tomorrow; hence the safe and sure religious foundation for all men is that laid down by Jesus, "The Spirit of truth . . . shall guide you into all the truth." A statement setting forth the teaching of a religious institution is essential, but compelling clauses should be omitted.

The Mosaic law had been framed for the benefit of the Hebrews, but their priesthood made it a hindrance to spiritual progress. Jesus was an iconoclast, and He made it His special business to break nearly every rule of action that the priests had evolved. For example, they had thirty-nine prohibitions in regard to the observance of the Sabbath. These were nearly all trivial, such as preparing food, riding on a beast, drawing water, carrying a burden, going on a journey; yet death was the penalty for transgression. Labor of any kind on the Sabbath was punishable by death. To roll grains of wheat in the hand was considered labor, so when the disciples of Jesus plucked the ears of grain the Pharisees said to Him: "Behold, why do they on the sabbath day that which is not lawful?" Then Jesus gave them a sermon on freedom from their narrow rules governing the Sabbath day; He ended with, "The sabbath was made for man, and not man for the sabbath."

The fact is that the Sabbath as an institution was established by man. God does not rest from His works every seventh day, and there is no evidence that there has ever been a moment's cessation in the activity of the universe. Those who stickle most for Sabbath-day observance are met on every hand by the evidence of perpetual activity on the part of Him whom they claim to champion.

We are told that trees, flowers, planets, suns, stars, and sidereal systems are the work of God; that it is God who sustains and governs, controls and directs them. Yet trees, flowers, planets, suns, and stars are active the first day and the seventh day of the week, just the same as on other days.

It would seem proper that, if God ordained a certain day of rest and rested on that day Himself, as is claimed, He should give some evidence of it in His creations; but He has not done this, so far as anybody knows. The truth is that Divine Mind rests in a perpetual Sabbath, and that which seems work is not work at all. When man becomes so at-one with the Father-Mind as to feel it consciously, he also recognizes this eternal peace, in which all things are accomplished. He then knows that he is not subject to any condition whatsoever and that he is "lord even of the sabbath."

Man can never exercise dominion until he knows who and what he is and, knowing, brings forth that knowledge into the external by exercising it in divine order, which is mind, idea, and manifestation. Jesus horrified the Jews by healing the sick, plucking grain, and performing other acts, which to them were sacrilegious, on the Sabbath day. The Jews manufactured these sacred days and observances, just as our Puritan fathers made life a burden by their rigid and absurd laws governing the religious acts of the people. For centuries the Jews had been binding themselves to the wheel of religious bigotry, and the Puritans accomplished a like task in a shorter time. The length of time was the only difference.

But Jesus knew all the exacting ecclesiastical rules to be man-made. "He himself knew what was in man," and He attempted to disabuse those benighted minds of their error. He tried to make them understand that the Sabbath was made for man, not man for the Sabbath. They had wound themselves up in religious ceremonies until their ecclesiastical machinery dominated every act of their lives. Not only were they subjects of their sacred law, but they were its absolute slaves.

It was the mission of Jesus to break down this mental structure, which had been reared through ages of blind servitude to form and ritual. The Mosaic law had been made so rigid that it held the Jews in its icy bonds to the exclusion of all reason and common sense. Jesus saw this, and He purposely overstepped the bounds of religious propriety in order that He might more effectively impress upon them the fact that the old Mosaic dispensation was at an end. He told them that He did not come to break the law, but to fulfill it. He was speaking of the true law of God, and not their external rules of sacrifice, penance, Sabbath observance, and the like. He knew that these rules were of the letter—purely perfunctory; that they were in reality hindrances to the expression of the inner spiritual life.

Man cannot grow into the understanding of Spirit,

nor be obedient to its leading, if he is hampered by external rules of action. No man-made law is strong enough, or true enough, or exact enough, to be a permanent guide for any one.

If in your path toward the light you have fixed a point of achievement the attainment of which you think will satisfy you, you have made a limitation that you must eventually destroy. There is no stopping place for God; there is no stopping place for man.

If the church goes back to Moses and the old dispensation, ignoring the lessons of Jesus Christ, it is no guide for you. If you want to be His disciple, you must unite your spirit with His.

Paul, with his dominant beliefs in the efficiency of the old way, at times loaded those beliefs upon the free doctrine of Jesus, but that is no reason why you should be burdened with them. You can never be what the Father wants you to be until you recognize that you stand alone, with Him as your sole and original guide, just as much alone as if you were the first and only man. You can hear His Word when you have erased from your mind all tradition and authority of men, and His Word will never sound clearly in your mind until you have done this.

It is not necessary that you despise the scriptures of the Jews, of the Hindus, or of any people, but you are to take them for what they are—the records of men as to what their experiences have been in communing with the omnipresent God. As Jesus said to the Pharisees: "Ye preach the scriptures, because ye think that in them ye have eternal life; and these are they which bear witness of me; and ye will not come to me, that ye may have life." From all sacred writings you can get many wonderfully helpful hints as to the work of God in the minds of men. You should treasure all pure words of Truth that have been written by brothers in the Spirit, yet they are not authority for you nor should you be moved to do anything simply because it is written in the Scriptures as a law of God for the specific guidance of man.

Mortal man loves to be dominated and whipped into line by rituals and masters, but divine man, the man of God, oversteps all such childish circumscribings and goes direct to the Father for all instruction.

It is your privilege to be as free as the birds, the trees, the flowers. "They toil not, neither do they spin," but are always obedient to the divine instinct, and their every day is a Sabbath. They stand in no fear of an angry God, though they build a nest, spread a leaf, or open a petal, on the first day or on the seventh day. All days are holy days to them. They live in the holy Omnipresence, always doing the will of Him who sent them. It is our duty to do likewise. That which is instinct in them is conscious, loving obedience in us. When we have resolved to be attentive to the voice of the Father and to do His will at any cost, we are freed from the bondage of all man-made laws. Our bonds—in the form of some fear of transgressing the divine law—slip away into the sea of nothingness, and we sit on the shore and praise the loving All-Good that we are never more to be frightened by an accusing conscience or by the possibility of misunderstanding His law.

But we are not to quarrel with our brother over observance of the Sabbath. If he insists that the Lord should be worshiped on the seventh day, we shall joyfully join him on that day; and if he holds that the first day is the holy day, we again acquiesce. Not only do we do God's service in praise, song, and thanksgiving on the seventh day and the first day, but also on every day. Our souls are open to God every moment. We are ever ready to acknowledge His holy presence in our heart; it is a perpetual Sunday with us. We are not satisfied with one day out of the seven set aside for religious observance, but, like the birds, the trees, and the flowers, we join in a glad refrain of thanksgiving in and out of season. When we work and when we sleep we are ever praising the holy Omnipresence that burns its lamp of love perpetually in our heart and keeps forever the light of life before us on our way.

This is the observance of God's holy day that the divinely wise soul forever recognizes. It is not in churches nor in temples reared by man in any form, that he finds communion with the Father. He has found the true church, the heaven within himself. There he meets the Father face to face; he does not greet Him as one removed to a distant place, to whom he communicates his wishes through some prophet or priest, but each for himself goes to the Father in closest fellowship.

"God so loved the world, that he gave his only begotten Son, that whosoever believeth on him should not perish, but have eternal life." This does not mean that a personal man, named Jesus of Nazareth, was sent forth as a special propitiation for the sins of the world, or that the only available route into the Father's presence lies through such a person. It simply means that God has provided a way by which all men may come consciously into His presence in their own souls. That way is through the only begotten Son of God, the Christ consciousness, which Jesus demonstrated. This consciousness is the always present Son of the Father, dwelling as a spiritual seed in each of us and ready to germinate and grow at our will. The Son of God is in essence the life, the love, and the wisdom of the Father himself; through us the Son is made manifest as a living individuality. He cannot be killed out entirely; He ever glows at the center of our being as the *"light* which lighteth every man, coming into the world."

To believe on the Son is to come to His terms of expression. It is the simplest thing in the world. Just *believe* that He is the only begotten Son of the Father. Do not believe that there are other sons wiser than He is, and that from them you can get wisdom, guidance, and understanding, but know that He is indeed the only begotten Son.

This distinction is a vital point for you to apprehend, and when you have once apprehended it your journey back to the Father's house is easy. "No one cometh unto the Father, but by me," the only Son is constantly saying in your heart, and you must not ignore His presence if you would know the sweets of the heavenly home where the love of God forever burns its incense of peace, plenty, and contentment. Let Christ be formed in you, was Paul's admonition. This is not hyperbole or an abstraction, but a statement of a definite rule of procedure, which you can discover and prove by making terms with this indwelling Son of the Father. His terms are not severe. They are simply obedience, obedience.

Jesus of Nazareth found this inner flame and let it burn all through His body. It so lighted Him up that His presence warms all sin-sick souls to this very day.

But no one lives by reflection. You could not live a moment if it were not for this only begotten Son of the Father within you. So you cannot live and grow on the reflected light of Jesus of Nazareth. The only begotten Son of God must come forth in you as it did in Jesus. Then your life will be permanent, and the discords of the flesh will drop away forever; then will your Sabbath be revealed to you.

The redemptive, restorative, and regenerative work that the Christ of God did through Jesus is not ignored by Christian metaphysicians. However, the salvation of men from the sins of mortality was not accomplished by the man Jesus alone; it was through the power of the Christ in Jesus that God provided purified life and substance for the corruptible bodies of men. Jesus' body was used as the vehicle through which a fresh and pure life stream and a regenerative substance were made available to all those who will accept them. The redeemed substance of the body of the Lord is just as essential to full salvation as His blood. Also, this is a salvation that is to be attained here in the earth, and not after death. Jesus' body was metamorphosed or changed from the corruptible flesh of the average man to the incorruptible substance of divine man. When we eat and drink of His body we shall become like Him in body perfection. This process of restoration of the body of man to its original purity is the basis of divine or spiritual healing. The complete redemption of the body may not be accomplished in one incarnation, but whoever accepts the Christ as life and substance, and conforms to righteous living as taught by the Spirit of truth, will finally sit with Jesus on the throne of dominion over disease and death.

There is a law of spiritual and mental growth constantly at work in the mind, a law that is raising man from sense consciousness, or Egypt, to spiritual consciousness, or Canaan. Moses means "drawn out," and represents in Scripture symbology this progressive or drawing-out process, which works from within out. As applied to the universe, this upward trend of all things is called by material science the evolutionary law. In our spiritual interpretation we observe the working of the law in the individual, because by that method we can bring home the lesson. Through intelligent use of the hints given, we apply the lesson to ourselves with great profit.

Involution always precedes evolution. That which is involved in mind evolves through matter. Joseph down in Egypt portrays the involution in matter of a high spiritual idea. The spiritual idea attracted other ideas like it (Joseph's relatives), and they greatly multiplied in the land of Egypt. It is estimated that the children of Israel increased from a few score to at least two millions. This illustrates the fact that spiritual thoughts grow with tremendous rapidity in consciousness when they have Truth as a nucleus.

Yet these true thoughts, which have so greatly multiplied, are in slavery to the Egyptians (sense nature), and a special effort has to be made to free them. We have our high ideals, but because the temporal life seems so important those ideals are made to work in the most menial ways to carry on this passing show. A time comes, however, when we rebel at this tyranny; we rise up in so-called righteous indignation, and in violent ways we kill out the opposing sense nature, as Moses killed the Egyptian. But this is not the right way. We are not to be liberated by suppression of sense, or by violent overcoming, but by a steady step-by-step demonstration over every error. The Lord recognizes the rights of the physical man, and He hardens Pharaoh's heart that he may sustain for a season his rightful place in consciousness.

The fleeing of Moses to the wilderness represents

the discipline that we must undergo when we seek the exalted One. Horeb means "solitude"; that is, we have to go into the solitude of the within and lead our flock of thoughts to the back of the wilderness, where dwells the exalted One, the I AM, whose kingdom is good judgment. There we are in training forty years, or until we arrive at a four-sided or balanced state of mind. Then the light of intuition or flame of fire burns in our heart, yet it is not consumed—there is no loss of substance. In brain thinking there is a vibratory process that uses up nerve tissue, but in the wisdom that comes from the heart the "bush" or tissue is not consumed. This thinking in wisdom is "holy ground," or substance in its spiritual wholeness; that is, the idea of substance in Divine Mind. When this holy ground is approached by man he must take off from his understanding all limited thoughts of the Absolute—he must put his shoes off his feet.

It is at this wisdom center within us that God proclaims Himself to be the Father of fathers, the God of Abraham, Isaac, and Jacob; thus our real Father is revealed to us as Spirit.

In our communion in the silence with the light within us, the bondage of the higher to the lower is made clear to us, and the true way of release is indicated. We see the possibilities of man and the goodness of the "promised land," to which we can raise every thought. But Moses was very meek— we feel our inability, and we say, "Who am I, that I should go unto Pharaoh, and that I should bring forth the children of Israel out of Egypt?" Then we have the assurance that God's power is with us —"Certainly I will be with thee." It is in the recognition of the power and the presence of God that all our strength and all our ability lie. Jesus, the great spiritual master, said, "The Father abiding in me doeth his works."

All great structures are erected on firm foundations. Any one whom the Lord calls to a work will succeed in the end, if he lays his foundation deep and strong in spiritual understanding. This understanding is attained through meditation and study in the silence. Moses was forty years separated from the busy haunts of men, learning to know God "face to face."

In our silent meditations and prayers we must infuse into the inner mind realms the same energy that, used without, would make us notable in some worldly achievement. But unless we do this inner work and lay the foundation of strength and power in the subjective mind, we shall find ourselves in failing health when called upon for extra exertion in some great effort.

The angel of the Lord, the flame of fire, and the bush, are all within the consciousness of man, becoming manifest through interior concentration. The bush is a nerve center through which the universal life energy runs like electricity over a wire, making a light but not consuming. The angel is the presiding intelligence that is always present in every life action or function.

Man is first attracted by the phenomenal side of spiritual things; then, when he gives his attention for the purpose of knowing the cause, the Lord reveals Himself. When Moses turned aside and began to investigate, he found that he was on holy ground. The forces of Spirit at the center of man's body are so intense that the outer consciousness cannot stand the current and hold itself together; absolutely pure in essence, this inner fire must be approached by the pure spiritual thought. Removing the sandals is symbolical of taking all material concepts from the understanding.

The Spirit of the Lord has been evolving in the subconsciousness, incarnation after incarnation. This I AM was the moving factor in Abraham, Isaac, and Jacob—the Lord is present in all.

Egypt is strictly material consciousness. It pertains to the physical sense of life, the corporeal organism. Canaan is life and substance in a radiant state; here Spirit finds its natural expression. The thoughts that belong in the radiant body have become slaves of material sense, and the higher self, the Lord, would set them free. But to do this the higher understanding must become part of their consciousness. All things are created by and through certain states of mind or consciousness.

The higher spiritual consciousness is infused into the mortal or personal consciousness. Personal I must take on supreme I AM. When this is first experienced there is a feeling of inefficiency. But the Lord's promise to be present under all circumstances is a mighty inner assurance.

Christian metaphysicians have learned by experience the power of words and thoughts sent forth in the name of the supreme I AM. The word of the Lord spoken by naturally weak men has produced marvelous results, because they set their minds not upon their own weak ideas of man and his abilities, but upon the mightiness of the great I AM. The Lord God, speaking through them, does the work of the Master. "I speak not from myself: but the Father abiding in me [supreme I AM] doeth his works."

Moses and Pharaoh represent two forces at work in the consciousness—especially that part of it pertaining to the body. Moses represents the evolutionary force of new ideas that have grown in the subconsciousness; these forces struggle with the old states of limitation and material ignorance, trying to rise out of their depths into a higher life expression. The rising into a higher life is symbolized by the man Moses, whose name means "drawn out." As a child he was drawn out of the water, a negative yet universal condition of life evolution. Pharaoh represents the force that rules the body under the material régime. The Lord is the universal law, whose impulse is always upward and onward. It is found, by those who are undergoing the regenerative process that in the story of Moses the Scriptures symbolically describe, that these two forces are constantly at work in consciousness, one holding to old ideas and striving to perpetuate them in form, and the other idealizing the new and bending every effort to break away from material bondage and rise above its limitations. Paul says, "The flesh lusteth against the Spirit, and the Spirit against the flesh." Looking at it from the personal standpoint, we are likely to cry out in this struggle, "Who shall deliver me out of the body of this death?" But as philosophers, with an understanding of the law of change, we balance ourselves between these two forces and let them work out under the equilibrium of the universal preserver of all forms, the Lord.

Here is consolation for those who chafe under the whips and cords of the regenerative law. Because of their many defeats and the snail's pace at which they progress, they think that they are off the track. However, they are not. They will attain their good if they persevere and patiently wait upon the Lord. If the energy of Spirit were instantly poured into the body it would destroy the organism because of the impurities of the flesh, but, by and through the evolutionary adjustment of the natural man, the Spirit not only preserves but raises up the substance and life of the organism. The purpose of our spiritual thoughts (the Children of Israel) down in the body (Egypt) is to raise up the body—gradually to infuse into it a more enduring life and substance. At the same time our spiritual thoughts get the substance (corn) that is to sustain their existence in the world of phenomena.

When you affirm the spirituality of the body and yearn for release from its bondage, you are making demands upon Pharaoh. In fear that he will all at once lose his hold upon life, he hardens his heart, and sometimes the Lord, the universal law of equilibrium, hardens it for him. Then there seems a failure to attain that which you have tried to demonstrate. But a step has been taken in the evolution of the body, and you will find that you are gradually becoming stronger, both physically and spiritually.

There are climaxes in this refining trend of the consciousness, and in these we make a signal effort and realize a great uplift. "Jewels of silver, and jewels of gold" represent wisdom and love in an external sense, which are to be asked or demanded by the Children of Israel. (The word "borrow" in the Authorized Version is an error.) The meaning is that we are to affirm that all wisdom and all love, even in their most external manifestations, are spiritual. By so affirming we put Spirit into control both within and without ourselves, and do away with the external ruling power, which is the "first-born in the land of Egypt." The first-born of every state of consciousness is the personal *I*. When the flood of light from the universal is let in through our declaration of the one wisdom and one love, this *I* of every mortal state of consciousness is slain, and there is a "great cry throughout all the land of Egypt."

We may mentally have made our truest statements and seemingly complied with all the law, yet Pharaoh does not let our people go—there is no realization of freedom in the body consciousness. Another step is necessary, which is typified in the feast of the Passover.

In every change of consciousness on the physical plane, there is a breaking down of some cells and a building up of other cells to take their place. Mentally this is denial and affirmation, and this process in the body is the result of these two movements in the mind which have occurred at some previous period. We let go of the animal life and take hold of the spiritual by giving up consciously to this "passing over" process, which takes place when the old cells are replaced by the new. The lamb that is killed and eaten in the night represents giving up the animal life in the obscurity of the mortal body. The command is that the lamb shall be without spot or blemish, and be wholly eaten after being roasted with fire. This refers to the complete transmutation and surrender of the human life after it has been purified by the fires of regeneration. Fire represents the positive, affirmative state of mind, as opposed to the negative or watery state. The Children of Israel were commanded not to let the lamb be "sodden." "Sodden" is the Old English past participle of "seethe." We are not to allow the life in our organism to simmer and stew with the worries and negative words of mortality, but we must set it afire with strong words of absolute Truth.

This is to show us that there must be a physical as well as a mental sacrifice, and that "the whole congregation of the children of Israel" will join in it; that is, the whole consciousness of spiritual desire will acquiesce. Many metaphysicians think that it is not necessary to change the habits of the sense man —that one has only to keep one's thoughts right and the flesh will thereby be wholly regulated. But the Scripture teaches that there must be a conscious physical change before the complete demonstration in mind and body is manifest. Thoughts work themselves out in things, and we get the full result of their work only when we follow them consciously every step of the way and help them along. Watch your thoughts as they work their way through your organism, and, if you find that some pure thought of spiritual life is striving to free the life in the appetites and passions of your physical Egypt, help it by consciously elevating that life to the open door of your mind. This is typified by putting the blood of the lamb on the two side posts and on the lintel of the door of the house. Do not be afraid to express your inner life to the Lord, for only in perfect candor and childlike innocence can man come under the protection of the divine law.

So long as there is a hidden, secret use of God's life in our habits and ways that we are not willing that all should know, just so long will the bondage of Egypt's Pharaoh hold us in its clutches. The whole man must be pure, and his inner life must be made so open and free that he will not be afraid to blazon it upon the very doors of his house where all who pass may read. Then the Lord will execute His judgment, and those who have purified the life of the lamb of the body will escape the messenger or thought of death.

129

CHAPTER XI

※

Zeal—Enthusiasm

THE EGO, the free *I*, the imperishable and unchangeable essence of Spirit, which man is, chooses every state of consciousness and every condition in which it functions. It does not create the basic substances that enter into these mental structures, for these substances have been provided from the beginning, but it gives form and character to them in consciousness, as men build houses of lumber, stone, or whatever material they may choose in the manifest.

These mental states are all constructed under the dynamic power of the great universal impulse that lies back of all action—enthusiasm or zeal. Zeal is the mighty force that incites the winds, the tides, the storms; it urges the planet on its course, and spurs the ant to greater exertion. To be without zeal is to be without the zest of living. Zeal and enthusiasm incite to glorious achievement in every aim and ideal that the mind conceives. Zeal is the impulse to go forward, the urge behind all things. Without zeal stagnation, inertia, death would prevail throughout the universe. The man without zeal is like an engine without steam or an electric motor without a current. Energy is zeal in motion, and energy is the forerunner of every effect.

If you desire a thing, you set in motion the machinery of the universe to gain possession of it, but you must be zealous in the pursuit in order to attain the object of your desire. Desire goes before every act of your life, hence it is good. It is the very essence of good; it is God Himself in a phase of life. When they called Jesus good, He said: "Why callest thou me good? none is good save one, *even* God." So the universal desire for achievement, giving its mighty impulse to all things, is divinely good. Divine enthusiasm is no respecter of persons or things. It makes no distinctions. It moves to new forms of expression even that which appears corrupt. It tints the cheek of the innocent babe, gleams from the eye of the treacherous savage, and lights in purity the face of the saint.

Some have named this universal life impulse God, and have left the impression that it is all of God and that all the attributes of God-Mind are therefore involved as a conscious entity in every situation where life is manifest. In this they lack discrimination. God's Spirit goes forth in mighty streams of life, love, substance, and intelligence. Each of these attributes is conscious only of the principle involved in it and in the work that it has to do. Though it is man's mission to combine these inexhaustible potentialities under divine law, man is free to do as he wills. But the divine law cannot be broken, and it holds man responsible for the result of his labors. Man cannot corrupt the inherent purity of any of God's attributes, but he can unwisely combine them in states of consciousness that bring dissatisfaction and incompleteness to him. It is his privilege to learn the harmonious relations of all the chords of life and to arrange them on the staff of existence with such masterly art that no discord can be detected. Then life becomes to him a song of joy, and he absolutely knows that in its ultimate all is good.

Never repress the impulse, the force, the zeal welling up within you. Commune with it in spirit and praise it for its great energy and efficiency in action. At the same time analyze and direct its course. As zeal alone, it is without intelligence or discretion as to results. As Jesus taught His disciples and combined their various talents, so every man must grow in wisdom and zeal. You are not to repress but to guide the spirit of enthusiasm, which in co-operation with wisdom will bring you happiness and satisfaction.

Zeal is the affirmative impulse of existence; its command is, "Go forward!" Through this impulse man forms many states of consciousness that he ultimately tires of. They may have served a good purpose in their day in the grand scheme of creation, but as man catches sight of higher things zeal urges him forward to their attainment.

Let your zeal be tempered with wisdom. "The zeal of thy house hath eaten me up" means that the zeal faculty has become so active intellectually that it has consumed the vitality and left nothing for spiritual growth. One may even become so zealous for the spread of Truth as to bring on nervous prostration.

"Take time to be holy." Turn a portion of your zeal to do God's will to the establishing of His kingdom within you. Do not put all your enthusiasm into teaching, preaching, healing, and helping others; help your own soul. Many enthusiastic spiritual workers have let their zeal to demonstrate Truth to others rob them of the power to demonstrate Truth for themselves. Do not let your zeal run away with your judgment. Some persons get so fired with zeal when they first tackle a job that they quickly grow tired, and eventually get "fired" from every job that they tackle.

Watch the first pull of a giant freight locomotive; note how it slowly but steadily moves forward, almost by inches at first but gradually increasing, until its mile-long train swiftly disappears in the distance.

Man is a dynamo of pent-up power, but he needs judgment in its use. Even love (John), the "greatest thing in the world," is linked in the twelve-power integration of Jesus with James (judgment). Jesus called these two brothers "Sons of thunder," comparing the effect of their combined power to the tremendous vibrations set up by unrestrained electrical energy. Judgment says to Love, "Look before you leap." Do not let unselfish zeal and enthusiasm for the loved one run away with your judgment. Remember that these two are brothers and that you should sit on the throne of your I AM dominion, with Love on the right hand and Judgment on the left, judging the twelve tribes of Israel. In these symbols we see portrayed the poise and mastery of regenerated man, directing and disciplining all his thought-people in wisdom and in love.

Even doctors are beginning to take notice of the emotional contests that take place between love and wisdom in our nervous system. Some of them say that indigestion may be caused by the disturbance that our emotions cause in the delicate nerve aggregations at the solar plexus, and that permanent stomach troubles may result. Metaphysicians have always taught that the contending vibrations or "thunder" between love and wisdom cause not only acute but chronic diseases of stomach and heart.

Heart says, "I love," and Wisdom says, "But you can't have what you love"; contention follows, and night and day the nerves are pounded by the warring emotions.

Love disappointed may lower the vitality to the vanishing point, while some physical disease is blamed.

Innumerable combinations of thoughts and their attendant emotions are constantly sending their vibrations or "thundering" to various parts of the body through the nerve cables that lead out from the many ganglionic centers.

Jesus had two disciples named Simon, but they represent different talents or faculties of man's mind. Simon Peter represents receptivity from above, and Simon the Cananaean represents receptivity from below. Simon means "hearing" and Canaan means "zeal." The Canaanites dwelt in the lowlands, so we know that the faculty designated by Simon the

Cananaean has its origin in the body consciousness.

But the receptivity to, and the zeal for, the truth that were manifested by Simon the Cananaean were lifting him to spiritual consciousness. This is symbolized in Acts 1:13, where it is written, "And when they were come in, they went up into the upper chamber, where they were abiding." Among them is mentioned "Simon the Zealot."

To grow spiritually we should always be careful to exercise our zeal in spiritual ways. Sincere Christians are apt to fall into commercial ways in carrying forward the Lord's work. We should remember that Jesus said, "God is spirit: and they that worship him must worship in spirit and truth." When Jesus cast the money-changers out of the Temple His disciples remembered that it was written, "Zeal for thy house shall eat me up." In this act Jesus was casting the commercial bargaining thoughts out of His body temple. This is explained in the context, John 2:18. The Jews said, "What sign showest thou unto us, seeing that thou doest these things? Jesus answered and said unto them, Destroy this temple, and in three days I will raise it up. . . . But he spake of the temple of his body."

Whatever takes place in the world about us has its counterpart in some thought process in our body.

Every invention of man is a duplication of some activity in the human body. The explosion of gasoline in an automobile cylinder is copied from the explosion of nerve substance in the cell centers of the body. The nerve fluid is conducted to a nerve chamber, corresponding to an automobile combustion chamber, where it is electrified and the energy liberated. In the human body spiritual zeal, that is, enthusiasm, electrifies the nerve substance, which breaks forth into energy.

Thoughts build nerve and brain centers that serve as distributors of the vital substance manufactured in the body. The vitamins in the food that we eat are stored up by the body chemistry and liberated in thought and action.

Every thought and emanation of mind and soul liberates some of this stored substance. We, the controlling intelligence, with our conscious mind direct these processes in a manner quite similar to that employed by the driver of an automobile.

An automobile driver should be familiar with the mechanism of his car. But in the great majority of cases the driver knows merely enough to perform a few mechanical motions, and the car does the rest.

So the mass of humans know but little about the delicate mind-and-body interaction. They perform a few necessary superficial acts, call in the doctor when anything goes wrong, and in the end dump the old "boat" at the junk pile.

Extraordinary zeal in the accomplishment of some ideal develops what is called genius. Jesus of Nazareth was undoubtedly the greatest genius that this earth has ever developed. He is not usually named among the geniuses of the earth, because He was a genius of such transcendental character that He is classed with the gods. He did manifest the mind of

God as no other has ever done, yet He was a man, and herein lies His genius:

In His humanity He developed extraordinary ability in spiritual wisdom, love, and power. There have been men who have told us about God, but none who have demonstrated the wisdom and power of God as Jesus did. His zeal in doing the will of God made Him a spiritual genius in human form.

Like others who manifest original genius, Jesus got His genius from within. He was not known to have been taught in the theological schools of His day, yet He exhibited a mental acumen and under-standing of religion that astonished His associates. They exclaimed in effect, "Where did this man get wisdom, never having studied."

Genius is the accumulated zeal of the individual in some chosen field of life action. The idea that God has arbitrarily endowed some persons with abilities superior to others' is not good logic, and makes God a partisan. God has no favorites, not-withstanding the fact that the Scriptures sometimes so interpret Him. "God is no respecter of persons." "This is my beloved Son, in whom I am well pleased," is the ideal or spiritual man, the Messiah, the Christ man, who is the pattern given to every man to follow.

However, we see on every hand evidences of pro-nounced diversity in human character, and, looking at life superficially, we think that God has given advantages in mind, body, and affairs to some souls that He has not given to others.

But what we see with the eye of flesh is only the physical manifestation of man. The spirit and soul must be taken into consideration and become a factor in our reasoning before we can know a man and properly estimate the whole man.

The body represents but one third of man's being. Man is spirit, soul, and body. The spirit is that in man which says I AM, and has existed from eternity. Spirit is potential man—soul is demonstrated man. Soul is man's memory, conscious and subconscious. We have carried along in our subconscious mind the memory of every experience that we have had since we began to think and act for ourselves. The soul is the mind, and the mind is the man.

The race to which we belong on this planet began thinking and acting in self-consciousness many millions of years ago. God alone knows the exact age of every soul. Jesus said, "The very hairs of your head are all numbered."

Every experience, every achievement, every failure, and every success is remembered by the soul and stored up in the subconscious mind. A new soul is not created with every physical birth. A physical birth simply means that a soul that died physically is taking on another body. Every soul inhabiting this earth and the psychic realms immediately surrounding it has gone through this process of dying and being reincarnated many times. You who read these lines have had experience as a thinking, free-acting soul for millions of years, instead of the score or three score that mortal man usually counts. Emerson said, "Be not deceived by dimples and curls; that child is a thousand years old."

Then the question arises, "Do we always get the fruit of our earthly acts in some future earthly life?" Certainly, "Whatsoever a man soweth, that shall he also reap." Here in this earth is the place of harvest. When a soul relinquishes its hold on its brain and nervous system, it gives up the only avenue through which it can adequately express itself.

So death is the great enemy to be overcome, as taught in Scripture. Death came into the world through Adamic ignorance, and it must go out through Christ understanding.

Genius is the breaking forth of the accumulated achievements of a soul in that field of activity for which it has been very zealous in many incarnations. Mozart at the age of four played the organ without instruction. Where did he get such marvelous musical ability? A history of his soul would show that he had cultivated music for ages, carrying from one incarnation to another his zeal for the harmony of sound, until he became the very soul of music.

The genius of Shakespeare was the accumulated experience of a soul that had been poet and philosopher since the "morning stars sang together."

Let no man think that he can retire from living. Do not shirk the responsibilities of life. You have made them and you can unmake them. A way of escape has been provided for every one of us. That way is to overcome the soul's mistakes by incorporating into mind and heart the attributes of the

139

Christ mind. "Travail until Christ be formed in you."

Simon the Zealot has his center or throne of dominion in the body at the base of the brain, named by physiology the medulla oblongata.

Let us think of man as a king having twelve sons or princes, who execute his will. Each of these princes has a throne, or brain and nerve center, from which he issues his orders and distributes his goods.

Jesus illustrated this in Matthew 19:28: "Verily I say unto you, that ye who have followed me, in the regeneration when the Son of man shall sit on the throne of his glory, ye also shall sit upon twelve thrones, judging the twelve tribes of Israel."

Simon the Zealot from his throne at the medulla imparts especial energy to the ears, eyes, nose, mouth, and sensory nervous system. When man enters into the understanding of his dominion, power, and directive ability in Christ, he educates his disciples, or sons, and shows them how to execute the law established in divine principle for man.

We all are kings in Christ. But with Him we must realize that "my kingdom is not of this world." Our dominion is over our own thoughts, emotions, and passions.

Our disciples will do what we tell them and continue to do it after they have been sufficiently instructed and assisted in the use of the Word.

Remember that mind rules in both the within and the without, the visible and the invisible, the high and the low.

To help Simon the Zealot do his work, center

your attention for a moment at the base of your brain and quietly affirm that infinite energy and intelligence are pouring forth in zeal—enthusiasm. Then follow in imagination a set of motor nerves that lead out from the medulla to the eyes, affirming all the time the presence and power of energy and intelligence now manifesting in your eyes.

For the ears affirm energy and intelligence, adding, *"Be you open."*

For the nose affirm energy and intelligence, adding, *"The purity of Spirit infolds you."*

For the mouth carry the life current to the root of the tongue, with the thought of *freedom.*

At the root of the tongue is situated the throne of another disciple, Philip. When you carry the zeal current from its medulla center and connect it with the throne of Philip, a mighty vibration is set up that affects the whole sympathetic nervous system. In this treatment you will strengthen your voice, revitalize your teeth, and indirectly impart energy to your digestion.

It was at Cana of Galilee, the nerve center in the throat, that Jesus turned water into wine. Metaphysically this miracle is accomplished when we in spirit realize that the union (wedding) of the fluid life of the body with the spiritual life at this power center makes a new element, symbolized by wine.

When the chemistry of the body and the dynamics of the mind are united, a third element is brought forth, and man feels that, "in Christ, *he is* a new creature."

141

CHAPTER XII

⌖

Renunciation

ALL CHRISTIANS who have had experiences variously described as "change of heart," "salvation," "conversion," and "sanctification" will admit that, before they experienced the great change of consciousness represented by these names, they had been "convicted of sin" or had determined to give up the ways of the world and do the will of God. The sinners most open to reform are those who sin in the flesh. The hardest to reach are the self-satisfied moralists or religionists. Jesus said to such, "Verily I say unto you, that the publicans and the harlots go into the kingdom of God before you." One who is living up to man-made morals or religious standards is not repentant, and he makes no room in his mind for new and higher ideals of life and Truth. Unless our repentance is accompanied by sacrifice we are still in our sins. "Apart from shedding of blood there is no remission." The blood represents the life, and when the life of the flesh is given up, the beasts of the body are literally killed and their blood or life carries away the dead cells. This was symbolically illustrated by Jesus when He sent the demons or evils into the swine (Matt. 8:32).

A change of mind effects a corresponding change

in the body. If the thoughts are lifted up, the whole organism is raised to higher rates of vibration. If the system has been burdened with congestion of any kind, a higher life energy will set it into universal freedom. But there must be a renunciation or letting go of the old thoughts before the new can find place in the consciousness. This is a psychological law, which has its outer expression in the intricate eliminative functions of the body.

As the physiologist studies the body, so the metaphysician studies the mind. It is true that some metaphysicians are not careful students. They often jump to conclusions, just as the ancient physiologists made wild guesses about the character of the bodily organs; but the majority of those who work with the inner forces get an understanding that conforms in fundamentals to the discoveries of other metaphysicians in the same field of work. The careful modern metaphysician does not arrive at his conclusions through speculation; he analyzes and experiments with the operations of his own mind until he discovers laws that govern mind action universally.

All those who go deep enough into the study of the mind agree perfectly on fundamentals, one of which is that the universe originated in mind, was projected into action by thought, and is being sustained by mind power. Self-analysis reveals the manner in which the individual mind acts, and this action is the key to all action in the small and the great, in the microcosm and the macrocosm, in man and in God. Another point of agreement is that thoughts are things, that they are ideas projected into form, partaking of the nature of the thinker.

Metaphysicians make a sharp distinction between the realm of ideas, which is Spirit, and the realm of thought, which is soul. Thoughts act in a realm just above, around, and within the material. They have but one degree more of freedom than matter. Thoughts have a four-dimensional capacity, while things have but three. Yet thoughts are limited to the realm in which they function, and man's consciousness, being made up of thoughts, is of like character. Thus it is possible to overload the mind, as one overloads the stomach. Thoughts must be digested in a manner similar to the way in which food is digested. An eagerness to gain knowledge without proper digestion and assimilation ends in mental congestion. The mind, like the bowels, should be open and free. It is reported that Lyman Beecher said to a friend, whom he was bidding good-by, "Worship God, be even-tempered, and keep your bowels open." It is found by metaphysicians that praise and thanksgiving are laxatives of efficiency and that their cleansing work not only frees the mind of egotism but also cleanses the body of effete matter.

Thoughts are things; they occupy space in the mental field. A healthy state of mind is attained and continued when the thinker willingly lets go the old thoughts and takes on the new. This is illustrated by the inlet and the outlet of a pool of water. Stop the inlet, and the pool goes dry. Close the natural outlet, and the pool stagnates, or, like the Dead Sea, it crystallizes its salts until they preserve everything that they touch.

The action of the mind upon the body is, in some of its aspects, similar to that of water upon the earth. Living old thoughts over and over keeps the inlet of new thoughts closed. Then begins crystallization—which materia medica has named arteriosclerosis. The cause is supposed to be some other disease, such as syphilis, which is classed as one of the most important of the primal causes of arteriosclerosis. Metaphysicians recognize syphilis as secondary in the realm of effects, and they ask, "What causes syphilis?" The cause is the uncontrolled enjoyment of sex sensation without asking or caring to know the object of that function in human consciousness. It would seem that in this respect the animals were under better discipline than men and women.

The enjoyment of the pleasures of sensation without wisdom's control may be compared to riding in a runaway automobile for the pleasure of the swift pace, wholly disregarding the crash that is sure to follow. But to take away man's freedom would delay his attaining the "son of God" degree, which is open to him when he learns to make a lawful use of the attributes of Being; consequently he must acquire more wisdom and self-control. Tuberculosis, syphilis, cancers, tumors, and the many other ills of the flesh are evidences that nature has been outraged and is protesting and striving to free itself from its unhappy condition.

Every cell of the body is enveloped in soul or thought, and its initial impulse is to conform to the divine-natural law. When this law is not observed by the will of man and cells are reduced to the slavery of lust, they combine with other cells of like condition, and, rather than submit longer to the debased condition, they destroy the organism. But the destruction of the cell as matter does not destroy it on the mental plane; the mental entity survives, and again seeks to carry out the great law of soul evolution that was implanted in it from the beginning. Thus the repeated incarnations of the soul— not only of the soul cell but of the great aggregation of cells known as man—are found to be a fact that explains the continuity of traits of mind and body handed down from generation to generation. It is not in the flesh that we inherit, but in the thoughts of the flesh. The flesh has returned to dust, but its memories endure until a higher mind power cleanses and lifts them to purer states of consciousness.

It is related in Genesis that when fleeing from the cities of Sodom and Gomorrah, which God was destroying, Lot's wife looked back, and "became a pillar of salt." Salt is a preservative, corresponding to memory. When we remember the pleasures of the senses and long for their return, we preserve or "salt" the sense desire. This desire will manifest somewhere, sometime, unless the memory is dissolved through renunciation. The desire for sensation in the flesh in one incarnation may be expressed in the next in a strong desire for personal love. Having become subconscious, it works in the subcenters of the organism in a fever of anxiety to attain its object, and it may be named consumption, or some other cell-consuming disease.

Modern medical science has traced nearly all the ills of the body to micro-organisms. The popular remedy is to introduce into the body germs much like the disease germs but of weakened power. The body, thereupon, in self-defense generates in the blood stream that which counteracts or neutralizes the disease, and renders the body immune to severe attack. If the patient is to continue to be immune, it logically follows that he must continue to have the disease germs in his system, because if they should desert him he would again be open to attack. Typhoid fever is quieted, or forestalled, by turning loose in the system good-natured typhoid germs. But the cause is not removed, and some who follow up such cases say that serums are spreading various forms of disease, and in various ways making the human family less virile. The writer knows of one instance where a healthy boy was vaccinated. A few months later he was attacked by tuberculosis of the hip, which the doctors said was caused by impure blood. All of this goes to show that the right kind of serum has not yet been discovered by medical science and that diseases are not cured by serums but are merely diverted, and eventually break out in other forms.

We see that such bacteriologists as Koch and

Pasteur have merely a clue to the real serum, which is the new life stream opened to man by Jesus Christ. It is true that the bodies of men are being destroyed by disease germs and that the palliative methods of bacteriology may enable us to live a little longer in the body, but until the Christ remedy is applied no real healing has been done. Destructive germs are the creations of destructive thoughts, and until the specific thought is found, physicists will continue to search for the healing serum. Their search is evidence that such a serum exists.

Destructive thinking separates soul and body, and, when the separation is complete, bacteria take up the work and distribute the body wreckage over the earth. If the body were left intact, this planet would soon become the abode of mummies, and the dead would crowd out the living. Then, so long as people continue to die, it is well that microbes make their bodies of some use.

> Imperious Caesar, dead and turn'd to clay,
> Might stop a hole to keep the wind away.

When the body becomes locally infested with bacterial thoughts and separates from the higher self, a forced removal of the adverse colony, by surgery, sometimes gives at least temporary relief. Man is the dominant thinking and character-giving force of the earth, and he has made it a place of desolation when it should be a paradise. Because of his lust, anger, arrogance, and ignorance, man has been tormented by pests, storms, and earthquakes.

Tradition says that in the dim past this planet's mental atmosphere was charged with the thoughts of men and women who exercised the power of mind in lust, arrogance, and ambition, until extreme measures had to be resorted to by the planetary God.

This story (which is merely a legend) relates that perversion of nature and her innocent life energies began cycles ago, when man in the first exuberance of psychic power built up a priestly hierarchy in the ancient continent of Atlantis. These masters of black magic dominated the world and dispossessed the cosmic mind. Extraordinary measures of safety for the whole race became necessary, and the higher powers planned and carried out the destruction of the continent Atlantis and all its people. The very soil of the continent which these occultists occupied had become saturated with lust and selfishness, and it was condemned as unfit to remain a part of the parent planet. The corrupted soil was scooped out of what is now the Atlantic Ocean and thrown off into space, where it became the lifeless mass known as the moon. The earth reeled like a drunkard under this terrible surgical operation, and still wabbles out of true perpendicular, the result of the shock and of the removal of so large a part of its body. Before this catastrophe occurred, a tropical climate extended to the very poles. The remains of tropical plants and animals are found in the frigid zones today, mute evidences that a great and sudden change has at some time taken place in the planet's relation to the sun. The withdrawal of warmth from the poles resulted in an unnatural coldness that congealed rain into snow and ice, which slowly piled up at the poles until they capped the earth to a great depth. This brought about the great glacial period, which lasted thousands of years, a reminder of which we get in icy blasts from the north, with months of cold and snow. However, the earth is slowly regaining its equilibrium and will in due season be restored to its pristine golden age, and all the desert places will bloom as the rose. So runs the tradition.

But how about the states of consciousness that man has built up and from which he would be free? No one can play fast and loose with God. What one builds one must care for. What man forms that is evil he must unform before he can take the coveted step up the mountain of the ideal. Here enters the factor that dissolves the structures that are no longer useful; this factor in metaphysics is known as denial. Denial is not, strictly speaking, an attribute of Being as principle, but it is simply the absence of the impulse that constructs and sustains. When the ego consciously lets go and willingly gives up its cherished ideals and loves, it has fulfilled the law of denial and is again restored to the Father's house.

As all desire is fulfilled through the formative word, so all denial must be accomplished in word or conscious thought. This is the mental cleansing symbolized by water baptism. In a certain stage of his problem man makes for himself a state of consciousness in which selfishness dominates. Personal selfishness is merely an excess of self-identity. This inflation of the ego must cease, that a higher field of action may appear. One who has caught sight of higher things is desirous of making unity with them. That unity must be orderly and according to the divine procession of mind. One who is housed in the intellect through desire may be ushered into the realm of Spirit by zeal. The first step is a willingness to let go of every thought that holds the ego on the plane of sense. This willingness to let go is symbolical of John the Baptist's crying in the wilderness, denying himself the luxuries of life, living on locusts and wild honey, and wearing skins for clothing.

The personalities of Scripture represent mental attitudes in the individual. John the Baptist and the Pharisees symbolize different phases of the intellect. John is willing to give up the old and is advocating a general denial through water baptism—mental cleansing. The Pharisees cling to tradition, custom, and Scripture, and refuse to let go. John represents the intellect in its transition from the natural to the spiritual plane. The Pharisees have not entered upon this transition, but cling to the old and defend it by arguments and Scripture quotations. Jesus, who represents the spiritual consciousness, does not take the Pharisees into account as a link in His chain, but of John He says: "Among them that are born of women there hath not arisen a greater than John the Baptist: yet he that is but little in the kingdom of heaven is greater than he." Jesus recognizes that the mental attitude represented by John is a prophecy of greater things, in fact the most desirable mental condition

151

for the intellect on its way to attainment, yet not to be compared with the mental state of those who have actually come into the consciousness of Spirit.

Every soul that cries out for God is John the Baptist crying in the wilderness. You who are satiated with the ways of the flesh man, and are willing to give up his possessions and pleasures, are John. The willingness to sacrifice the things of sense starts you on the road to the higher life, but you do not begin to taste its sweets until you actually give up consciously the sense things that your heart has greatly desired.

There are many phases of this passing over from John to Jesus, and some involve unnecessary hardships. The ascetic takes the route of denial so energetically that he starves his powers instead of transforming them. Some Oriental suppliants for divine favor castigate their flesh in many ways, starve their bodies, slash their flesh, and then salt it; they maltreat the body until it becomes a piece of inanimate clay that the soul can vacate until the birds build their nests in the hair of its head. This is Oriental denial, atrophy of the senses. Some Occidental metaphysicians are trying to imitate these agonizing methods of soul discipline, but in the mind rather than in the body.

John the Baptist stands for the mental attitude that believes that because the senses have fallen into ignorant ways they are bad and should be killed out. There is a cause for every mental tangent, and that which would kill the sense man, root and branch, has the thought of condemnation as its point of departure from the line of harmony. In John it seemed a virtue, in that he condemned his own errors, but this led to his condemnation of Herod, through which he lost his head. We learn from this that condemnation is a dangerous practice from any angle.

The intellect is the Adam man that eats of the tree of good and evil. Its range of observation is limited, and it arrives at its conclusions by comparison. It juggles with two forces, two factors— positive and negative, good and evil, God and devil. Its conclusions are the result of reasoning based on comparison, hence limited. The intellect, judging by appearances, concludes that existence is a thing to be avoided. The intellect, beholding the disaster and the misery wrought by the misuse of men's passions, decides that they should be crushed out by starvation. This is the origin of asceticism, the killing out, root and branch, of every appetite and passion, because in the zeal of action they have gone to excess.

Yet John the Baptist has a very important office in the development of the soul from intellectual to spiritual consciousness. As Jesus said:

"This is he, of whom it is written,
Behold, I send my messenger before thy face,
Who shall prepare thy way before thee."

Thus John the Baptist is the forerunner of Spirit. He stands for that perception of Truth which prepares the way for Spirit through a letting go of narrow ideas, and a laying hold of broad ones.

The ideas that you and your ancestors have held in mind have become thought currents so strong that their course in you can be changed only by your resolute decision to entertain them no longer. They will not be turned out unless the ego through whose domain they run decides positively to adopt means of casting them out of his consciousness, and at the same time erects gates that will prevent their inflow from external sources. This is done by denial and affirmation; the denial always comes first. The John the Baptist attitude must begin the reformation. Man must be willing to receive the cleansing of Spirit before the Holy Ghost will descend upon him. Whoever is not meek and lowly in the presence of Spirit is not yet ready to receive its instruction.

This obedient, receptive state means much to him who wants to be led into the ways of the supreme good. It means that he must have but one source of life, one source of truth, and one source of instruction; he must be ready to give up every thought and every idea that he has imbibed in this life, and must be willing to begin anew, as if he had just been born into the world a little, ignorant, innocent babe. This means so much more than people usually conceive that it dawns upon the mind very slowly.

All who sincerely desire the leading of Spirit acquiesce readily in the theoretical statement of the necessity of humility and childlikeness, but when it comes to the detailed demonstration many are nonplused. This is just as true among metaphysicians as among orthodox Christians. Spirit will find a way to lead you when you have freely and fully dedicated yourself to God, and you will be led in a path just a little different from that of any one else. Your teaching has been in generalities, so when Spirit in its office as an individual guide shows you Truth different from that which you have been taught, you may object. If, for instance, you have been taught to ignore the body with all its passions and appetites, and Spirit in its instruction shows you that you are to recognize these appetites and passions as your misdirected powers, what are you going to do about it?

There can be but one course for the obedient devotee. If you have surrendered all to omnipresent wisdom, you must take as final what it tells you. You will find that its guidance is the right course for you and, in the end, that it was the only course that you could possibly have taken.

All things are manifestations of the good. Man in his spiritual identity is the very essence of good, and he can do no wrong. He can in his experience misuse the powers placed at his disposal by the Father, but he can do no permanent evil. He always has recourse to Spirit, which forgives all his transgressions and places him on the right road, a new man, when he willingly gives up his own way and as a little child asks to be led. Then comes the redemption of the appetites and passions, which the ignorant intellect has pronounced evil and has attempted to kill out by starvation and repression. This does not mean that the indulgence of appetites and passions is to be allowed in the old, demoralizing way, but it means that they are to be trained anew under the direction of Spirit.

John the Baptist represents the attitude of spiritual receptivity that awaits the higher way as a little child awaits the helping hand of a parent. It is not the arbitrary disciplinarian, but the loving, tender kindergarten teacher, that illustrates in visible life the intricate problems that perplex the mind. When man is receptive and obedient, giving himself unreservedly up to Spirit and receiving its guidance without antagonism, he is delighted with the possibilities that are disclosed to him in the cleansing of mind and body. He then begins to realize what Jesus meant when He said: "If any man would come after me, let him deny himself, and take up his cross, and follow me."

The cross is not a burden, as commonly understood, but is a symbol of the forces in man adjusted in their right relation. The body of Jesus was lifted up and nailed to the cross, which indicates that the physical man must be lifted into the harmony of Spirit and adjusted to its four-dimensional plane, represented by the four branches of the crosstree.

Man thinks in the fourth dimension, but his body, in its present fleshly consciousness, can express in three dimensions only. Hence we must cleanse our thoughts by denying materiality. Then the flesh will become radiant ether with power to penetrate all so-called material substance. But before this can be done the mind of the man must become John the

Baptist—it must be cleansed by the waters of denial, and the old material ideas must be put away forever.

If you are clinging to any idea that in any way prevents your eyes from seeing the millennium here and now, you are a Pharisee; you are crying, "Beelzebub," whenever you say "crank" of the one who has caught sight of the spiritual mountaintops now glistening in the sun of the new age.

John the Baptist is now moving swiftly among the children of men. His cry is heard in many hearts today, and they are following him in the wilderness of sense. But the bright light of the Christ still shines in Galilee, and they who are earnest and faithful shall see it and be glad.

Those who attempt to heal the body by injecting into it a new life stream from without are attempting to do in a material way what Jesus attained spiritually. The vitality of the race was at a low ebb at His advent; He saw the necessity of a larger consciousness of life, and He knew how to inoculate the mind of every one who would accept His method. In John 5:26 it is written, "For as the Father hath life in himself, even so gave he to the Son also to have life in himself." Life is spiritual, as every one admits who has tried to find it in a physical laboratory. No one has ever seen life in food or drink, but it is there in small degree, and it is through eating and drinking that the body absorbs the invisible life elements that physical science has named vitamins. The vitamin is the essential life within all forms and, being spiritual in character, must be spiritually

157

discerned. We feel life's thrill in our body; by raising this consciousness of life to Christ enthusiasm, we may come to such fullness of energy that the whole life stream will be quickened and the congestions in arteries and glands swept away. "I came that they may have life, and may have *it* abundantly."

All spiritual metaphysicians know that the body and the blood of Jesus were purified and that each cell was energized with original spiritual substance and life, until all materiality was purged away and only the pure essence remained. This vitamin, or essence of life and substance, was sown as seed in the whole race consciousness, and whoever through faith in Christ draws to himself one of these life germs becomes inoculated to that degree with Jesus Christ quality, and not only the mind but also the body is cleansed.

"He that soweth the good seed is the Son of man; and the field is the world." Like a seed planted in soil, the word or thought germ will multiply and bring forth after its kind. "He that abideth in me, and I in him, the same beareth much fruit: for apart from me ye can do nothing."

The disciple Thaddaeus, called also Lebbaeus, carries forward the work of elimination of error thoughts from the mind and of waste food from the body.

The nerve center from which the eliminative function directs the emptying of the intestines is located deep in the lower bowels.

This center is very sensitive to thoughts about

substance and all materiality. A gripping mental hold on material things will cause constipation. A relaxation of the mind and a loosening up of the grip on material possessions will bring about freedom in bowel action.

The prevailing ills of the abdominal region, constipation, tumors, and the like, are caused by constriction of the whole body energy.

The faculties centering in the head are responsible for this slowing down of the life forces. The will, operating through the front brain, controls the circulation of the life force in the whole organism. A tense will, set to accomplish some personal end, keys everything to that end and puts a limitation on the activity of every other function.

The set determination to succeed in some chosen field of action, study, profession, business, or personal ambition calls most of the body energy to the head and starves the other centers.

In our schools the minds of our children are crammed with worldly wisdom, and they are spurred on to make their grades, thus constantly forcing the blood to the head and depleting its flow to the abdomen.

This overflow to the will center causes enlarged adenoids, inflamed tonsils, sinus trouble, and other ills of the head, while the abdominal region suffers with constipation and general lack of vital action.

Some persons relax in sleep and thus give the body an opportunity to recoup its depleted energy. But if the eager pace is kept up night and day, the end is nervous prostration. The remedy is relaxation of will, the letting go of personal objectives.

The strife to get on in the world is responsible for most of the ills of the flesh. Worry or anxiety about temporal needs disturbs in the body the even flow of nature's all-providing elements. Jesus warned against the tension of anxiety when He said, "Be not anxious for your life, what ye shall eat, or what ye shall drink; nor yet for your body, what ye shall put on. Is not the life more than the food, and the body than the raiment?"

A divine law has been provided for man that will meet every need when it is observed. "Seek ye first his kingdom, and his righteousness; and all these things shall be added unto you."

So we find that relaxation of the tense abdomen depends upon relaxation of the tense will.

Give up your willfullness and ask that the divine will be done in you and in all your affairs. Jesus set aside His will that God's will might be done in Him. "Not my will, but thine, be done."

⌐⌐⌐⌐⌐

CHAPTER XIII

Generative Life

THE LAW of generation is undoubtedly the mystery of mysteries in human consciousness. Men have probed, with more or less success, nearly every secret of nature, but of the origin of life they know comparatively nothing. It is true that they have with chemical combinations simulated life, but the activity has been temporary only.

In the phenomenal world, life is the energy that propels all forms to action. Life in the body is like electricity in a motor. As the engineer directs and regulates the electricity in a motor, so the life in the body has its engineer. Life is not in itself intelligent—it requires the directive power of an entity that knows where and how to apply its force, in order to get the best results. The engineer of the life force in the body of man is the life ego; this is the consciousness of life in the organism.

The life ego is the most subtle and most variable of all the powers of man. It is an animal force, and is designated in the Bible allegory as one of the "beasts of the field." It presides over the life and generative function of the body, and because of its tendency to separate and segregate itself from the other bodily functions, it is called the "adversary." It is not essentially evil, but because of its place as the central pole of all bodily activity, its tendency is to centralize all action around its consciousness.

In its divine-natural relation, the life ego has its positive pole in the top head, which is the "heaven" of man's consciousness. When the personality gets active and begins to exercise in the higher or spiritual forces, the life ego becomes inflated with its own importance and falls from heaven (top head) to earth, or front brain. When the seventy whom Jesus had indued with spiritual power returned, they proclaimed that even the demons were subject to them. Then Jesus said, "I beheld Satan as lightning fall from heaven." Jesus was evidently quoting Isaiah, who wrote in the 14th chapter of his book (King James Version):

How art thou fallen from heaven, O Lucifer, son of the morning! *how* art thou cut down to the ground, which didst weaken the nations!

For thou hast said in thine heart, I will ascend into heaven, I will exalt my throne above the stars of God: I will sit also upon the mount of the congregation, in the sides of the north:

I will ascend above the heights of the clouds; I will be like the Most High.

Yet thou shalt be brought down to hell, to the sides of the pit.

Jesus warned the seventy not to rejoice over their spiritual power, and added, "but rejoice that your names are written in heaven."

In order to give man a body having life in itself, God had to endow him with a focal life center, located in the generative organs. This center of activity in the organism is also the seat of sensation, which is the most subtle and enticing of all factors that enter into being. But these qualities (sensation and generation) were necessary to man's character, and without them he would not have been the complete representative, or image and likeness, of God.

God does not tempt man to break His law, but a great creative plan is being worked out in which the Deity is incarnating itself in its creation. This incarnation is called the Son of man; in man a wonderful being is in process of creation. This being is spiritual man, who will be equal with God, when he overcomes, or handles with wisdom and power, the faculties of the body. The body is the Garden of Eden.

What metaphysicians most need is a comprehension of the factors that go to make up consciousness. This requires discrimination, judgment, and self-analysis.

We talk glibly about God as life, love, intelligence, and substance, and about man as His manifestation, but when we come to describe that manifestation we "lump it off" as the product of thought.

What we now need to know is how thought groups the different attributes of Being, for upon this combination depends the bringing forth of the ideal man.

We must learn to watch our consciousness, its impulses and desires, as the chemist watches his solutions. Man forms his own consciousness from the elements of God, and he alone is responsible for the results.

Consciousness is a deep subject, and to go into it exhaustively would require the writing of many books. Concisely stated, three great factors enter into every consciousness—intelligence, life, substance. The harmonious combination of these factors requires the most careful attention of the ego, because it is here that all the discords of existence arise.

In Scripture the divine life combined with divine substance is termed "the Lamb of God." This phrase carries the symbology of the Lamb's purity, innocence, and guilelessness. Its nature is to vivify with perpetual life all things that it touches. It knows only to give, give unceasingly and eternally, without restraint. It does not carry wisdom; that is another quality of Being, which man comprehends from a different part of his consciousness.

The pure life of God flows into man's consciousness through the spiritual body, and is sensed by the physical at a point in the loins. This is the "river of water of life, bright as crystal, proceeding out of the throne of God and of the Lamb," referred to in the 22d chapter of Revelation.

Only those who have come into consciousness of the spiritual body can feel this holy stream of life. When the ego has found it, and laved in its cleansing currents, the ecstasy of Elysian realms is experienced. It cannot be described, because all the sensations of the mortal consciousness are coarse, compared with its transcendent sweetness and purity.

Many feel its thrills in part in silent meditation or in religious enthusiasm, and are temporarily stimulated by its exquisite vibrations. Just here is where the danger lies for those who have not brought out the other pole of Being—intelligence.

The ego, through its recognition of this life stream, sets it flowing to every faculty. Being by nature formless, the life stream takes the mold and character of that into which it is poured. It is the servant of the ego, the *I,* which man *is,* and through his failure to recognize the divine intelligence, which should show him how to use it in the right way, he blunders ahead in his ignorance, and the Lamb of God is slain from the foundation of the world.

The greatest danger of perversion lies in the direction of the carnal thought of sex, because it is there that this pure stream has been most foully polluted by ignorance. Sex sensation has made a broken cistern of man's consciousness; for generations the life stream has been turned into this receptacle, and lust has robbed the bodies of the whole race, making them mere shells, void of life. The failing eye, the deaf ear, the festering or withering flesh, all bear testimony to this perversion of God's life.

Yet men and women, otherwise applying good reason, continue their lustful practices and at the same time wonder why God does not give them more life.

They run here and there, seeking a restoring elixir for their failing powers; they call upon God for help, while they continue to squander His energy in lust.

Man is male and female, which are qualities of mind—love and wisdom. Every attempt to lower these divine attributes to the physical plane meets with disaster. It has been tried again and again in every age, and its votaries have always gone into demoralization if they persisted in trying to carry out their theories.

Yet it is not unlawful to have bodily sensations in regeneration. A change in ideas must necessarily produce a change in the body, and there is a perfect response in every center of consciousness when Spirit has been welcomed as the rightful inhabitant of the body. The marriage mystically spoken of in Scripture, and in other sacred books, takes place in the consciousness; it is a soul communion of the two-in-one, more sweet than that between the most harmoniously mated man and woman. This eliminates sex in its outer manifestation.

Persistently deny the carnal belief in sex, and realize that the life stream, which has been *turned outward* and named sex, is not of that character in its original purity, but is pure spiritual life.

You must cleanse this pure stream in its outward flow by destroying the carnal sense of sex. This can be done only by the power of your word. Do not kill out the life manifesting through your body by denying it away entirely; deny away the sense of impurity with which the animal ego has clothed it.

"To the pure all things are pure" does not mean that lasciviousness is pure, nor that the deifying of sexuality is pure. The purity is in knowing that behind and interior to these shadows is a pure substance that is of God, that must be seen by the eye of the pure. So long as your eye sees sex and the indulgence thereof, on any of its planes, you are not pure. You must become so mentally translucent that you see men and women as sexless beings—which they are in the spiritual consciousness.

Sex lust is the father of death. James, in the 1st chapter of his epistle, gives its history in these words: "Then the lust, which it hath conceived, beareth sin: and the sin, when it is full-grown, bringeth forth death."

Paul says, "to be carnally minded *is* death" (A. V.), and Jesus, in the 12th chapter of Mark, sums up the whole question in these words: "For when they shall rise from the dead [come out of the carnal consciousness], they neither marry, nor are given in marriage; but are as angels in heaven."

To desire to be instructed by God is the first step in exalting the inner life force. The sincere desire of the heart is always fulfilled by the divine law. All the woes of humanity have their root in disregard of law. Man has to deal with many factors in his "garden." The most "subtle" is the "serpent," or sense consciousness. It is not evil, as we have been taught to believe. The allegory given in the 3d chapter of Genesis plainly teaches that sensation (serpent) is a blind force, which should not be regarded as a source of wisdom. In its right relation the serpent stands upright on its tail, and forms the connecting link between the swift vibratory forces of Spirit and the slow vibrations of the flesh. "As Moses lifted up the serpent in the wilderness, even so must the Son of man be lifted up." In the body the spinal cord is the main cable of sensation, "the tree . . . in the midst of the garden," and its branches extend to all parts of the system. The "fruit" of this "tree," which the desire for sensation (serpent) urges man to eat, is the seminal fluid, which flows throughout the nervous system and is the connecting link between the mind and the body. When desire for sensation leads man to dissipate (eat) this precious "fruit" of the "tree" in his earthly garden, the whole nervous system is drained of its vitality and the spinal cord loses its capacity to conduct the higher life into the consciousness. Man feels a lack; he is "naked." Sensation is no longer a heavenly ecstasy but a fleshly sex vibration. It crawls on its "belly" and eats "dust" all the days of its life; that is, it functions in the driest, most lifeless part of man's being.

Yet sensation is a divine creation; it is part of the Lord God's formation and must find expression somewhere in the consciousness. This brings us to the root cause of that appetite which craves stimulants and goes to excess in seeking satisfaction in eating and in drinking. The cause is plainly to be seen when we understand the anatomy of mind and body. Sensation is seeking satisfaction through the appetites. By listening to this serpent of sense, man becomes sexually insane, a glutton and a drunkard.

The remedy is this: Turn away from the lusts of the flesh and seek God. Take up the problem from its spiritual standpoint. Sensation is a mental quality. It can be satisfied only by cultivation of the spiritual side of the nature. If you are a sexual drunkard, deny the power of this ungodly lust over you. Pray for the help to overcome, then affirm your own power and spiritual dominion over all the "beasts of the field" in your "garden." When you have obtained mastery over sexual intemperance, you will find the conquest of appetite easy. Simply deny all desire for material stimulants and affirm that you are satisfied with the stimulant of Spirit. Whenever the desire for the material stimulant manifests itself, say to it: *You are nothing. You have no power over me or over anybody else. I am Spirit, and I am wholly satisfied by the great flood of spiritual life that now fills my being.*

The result of sin is death; the truth of these words has been proved for ages. But when he was tempting her to disobey the divine law, the "adversary" said to Eve, "Ye shall not surely die." The tragedy of Eden is being enacted every day in every individual of the race, and death reigns in consequence. We may call it by any other name, but the breaking up of consciousness and the separation of spirit, soul, and body take place just the same. As Emerson said, "Behold a god in ruins." In face of the facts that God pronounced death to be the wages of sin and that the experience of the race has proved His words true, many people have listened to the "adversary" and have believed his lie. We hear them on every side saying, "Ye shall not surely die."

As the result of sin the whole human race is already "dead in trespasses and sins"; that is, the race is in a dying condition, which ends in the loss of the body. Death is not annihilation, because a resurrection has been promised.

To be "dead in trespasses and sins" is to lack realization of God, to be ignorant of His law and disobedient to it. When Jesus said, "I am the resurrection, and the life," He was telling of the power of the Christ mind to enter the mind and the body of man as quickening Spirit to awaken the whole consciousness to the knowledge of God. This resurrecting process is now going on in many people. It is a gradual change that brings about a complete transformation of the body through renewal of the mind. Spirit, soul, and body become unified with Christ mind, and body and soul become immortal and incorruptible. In this way death is overcome.

Those who insist that men do not die as a result of sin are building up a false hope of finding life after death. Those who understand that eternal life has been lost to the race through sin, and can be regained only through the resurrecting power of the Christ mind in the individual, are building on the eternal foundation of Truth. Every one must at some time come to understand that this statement is absolutely true: "He that hath the Son [consciousness of Christ] hath the life; he that hath not the Son of God hath not the life."

The belief that all the entities that speak through mediums are the spirits of dead people is not proved. The communications are so fragmentary, and usually so inferior to the natural ability of the supposed egos delivering them, that those of wide investigation doubt the authenticity of the authorship. No great literary production, great scientific discovery, or great sermon has ever come from spirits, yet the country in which it is claimed that they exist should contain all the wise people who have lived on the earth.

This theory of continuous progressive life after death contradicts the teachings of the Bible. God did not create man to die; death is the result of a transgression of law. Christianity teaches that man was created to live in his body, refining it as his thoughts unfold, and that the work of the Christ— the supermind in man—is to restore this state; that is, unite spirit, soul, and body here on earth. This must be fulfilled in the whole race, and every thought of death, or the possibility of leaving the body, must be put out of the mind.

Practical Christians object to thoughts that tend to separate soul and body, because by such thoughts is built up a consciousness that finally brings about that dissolution. It is a fact, well known to those who have deeply studied the law of Being, that death does separate spirit, soul, and body; that the communications received by spiritualists are but echoes of the soul, without its animating, inspiring, spiritual I AM; that this mentality that communicates falls in its turn into a sleep, or coma, even as the

171

body does, until the law again brings about a union with its I AM or higher self, and the building of another physical organism takes place. This process of repeated body building by the ego continues until the man, through Christ, makes a complete union of spirit, soul, and body here on earth. This union brings all of man's powers into conjunction, and what is mystically known as the Jesus Christ man, or redeemed man, appears.

We can easily see how illogical, unwise, and futile it is to teach that man can lay off his body as a worn-out garment and, by weakly giving up and dying, go on to higher attainment. We know whereof we speak, and we must proclaim this great truth taught by Jesus Christ: "Whosoever liveth and believeth on me [spiritual I AM] shall never die."

If God created man to die and go on to a spirit land to get his education, then it would be better for him to die in infancy and escape the hardships of life. Also, if death is part of God's law, we are defeating that law every time we attempt to escape death by trying to heal the body.

If man's birth as an infant a few years ago were the beginning of his existence, then God has performed a miracle and made an exception of man in the progressive law of development that is evident in all His other works.

The fact is—and it is well known to initiates—that spiritualists are in communication with the mentality of humanity, that is, the personal consciousness. Not having developed the superconscious mind, they do not understand the creative law. They function mentally and physically in a thought psychism that is mixed and uncertain. Their communications can all be explained in the action of the subconscious minds of the living, and the majority of mediums are uncertain as to whether they are moved by their own or some other mentality.

When man has brought his higher self into action he will see clearly the relation of spirit, soul, and body, in all phases of their action.

If you want to know all the mysteries of life, study life and put out of your mind every thought about death or the condition of the dead. Then through the law of thought formation you will build up in yourself such a strong consciousness of life that its negative (or absence) will ever be to you nonexistent. Jesus meant this when He said, "If a man keep my word, he shall never see death."

The desire to live does not cease when the body dies. The mind lives on, not in heaven or hell, but in the states of consciousness that it has cultivated in life. Mind does not change with a change of environment. Those who leave the body of matter find themselves in a body of ether, which does not respond to their desire for coarse sensations. Jesus taught in Luke 16:23 that the rich man who died was in "torment" in Hades. In the original language in which the Bible was written Hades was a term used to represent the unseen world. Those who have cultivated spiritual thoughts find themselves at death in an environment and in an ether body corresponding to their prevailing thoughts. But the very fact that they died proves that they gave up to the "adversary," that they did not attain the dominion, power, and authority of spiritual man. Consequently after a period of recreation and rest they will again take up active, overcoming life in a flesh body through reincarnation. So this process of life and death will continue until the ego overcomes sin, sickness, and death, and raises the body of flesh to the body of Spirit without the tragedy of death. "This corruptible must put on incorruption; this mortal must put on immortality."

Our theologians have not discerned man's life in its entirety—they have attempted to crowd into one physical incarnation the character that it has taken aeons to develop. As taught by Jesus, and by all spiritual teachers, the goal of man is the attainment of eternal life; the overcoming of physical death. The human race on this planet will continue to die and be reborn until it learns the law of right living, which will ultimate in a body so healthy that it will never die. Jesus demonstrated this, and He promised those who should follow Him in the regeneration that they would never see death if they should keep His words. Many Christians are getting this understanding—that they have not attained eternal life so long as they allow the body to continue in the corruption that ends in death, and they are earnestly beginning the appropriation, or eating and drinking, of the life and substance of the Lord's body, until He appears again in their regenerated organism.

174

QUESTION HELPS

For Students of

The Twelve Powers of Man

THE TWELVE POWERS OF MAN

CHAPTER ONE

1. What do Jesus' twelve disciples represent in man's spiritual ongoing?

2. What is symbolized by the first and second coming of Christ, as spoken of in the Scriptures?

3. How may the twelve disciples be likened to the heads of departments in an industrial plant?

4. What does Jesus represent in man's consciousness?

5. Name each disciple and the corresponding faculty represented.

6. Why was Peter (faith) called the first disciple?

7. Explain how a center may be baptized by the word of Spirit and given new power.

8. Why does the intellect deny that man can have knowledge of God?

9. How should the twelve powers of man be developed and expressed?

THE DEVELOPMENT OF FAITH

CHAPTER TWO

1. What does Abraham represent in man's consciousness?

2. Why must this faculty be abiding?

3. Why is faith put to a test?

4. Give the symbology represented by Abraham's offering of his son, Isaac.

5. Explain the law of giving and receiving.

6. What is symbolized by the "upper room" to which the Holy Spirit comes?

7. What is the difference between the prayer of supplication and the affirmative prayer?

8. What are the two attitudes of faith that are brought out? Explain.

9. Who was the first and greatest disciple of Jesus?

10. What does his name mean?

11. Why was his name changed after he became Jesus' disciple?

12. What is the difference between trust and real faith?

13. Why is the spoken word formative, but not always creative?

14. Where is the faith center in the body of man? How is it quickened?

15. What is the significance of a change of mind?

16. Explain how Jesus accomplished the mighty works credited to Him.

STRENGTH—STABILITY—STEADFASTNESS

CHAPTER THREE

1. Which one of Jesus' disciples symbolized strength in man's consciousness?

2. Wherein is the source of all things?

3. Why is man greater than all other expressions of Divine Mind?

4. What is the difference between the Jehovah man and the Adam man?

5. Explain God's creation of man as "male and female."

6. What does the "strong *man* fully armed," referred to by Jesus, represent in the natural man?

7. What does it represent in the regenerate man?

8. Explain the symbology brought out by the story of David and Goliath.

9. What does Samson symbolize in man's consciousness?

10. Explain the symbology of his being robbed of his hair by Delilah.

11. Why should man conserve the vital essence of his body?

12. Explain how one may renew the body through using the various brain centers.

13. How does creative law affect man's development?

14. Explain man's growth in consciousness through evolution.

15. Why is the Word of God likened unto a seed?

16. Why is Jesus Christ the Great Teacher?

WISDOM—JUDGMENT

CHAPTER FOUR

1. What are the twelve powers of man?

2. Where is the wisdom center in man's consciousness?

3. Name some attributes of wisdom.

4. Is knowledge of the negative side of good necessary to man's unfoldment?

5. Explain some of the functions of the solar plexus, and name its presiding ego.

6. What is man's first step in the regeneration?

7. Where is this step referred to in Scripture symbology?

8. How do we "call a disciple"? Give an example.

9. What is Christ?

10. Explain the lawful method of entering the kingdom of God.

11. Can man escape divine judgment? Why?

12. What part does spiritual judgment play in the working out of man's salvation?

13. Why are Peter, James, and John mentioned more than the other disciples?

14. Why was Andrew also among the first-called disciples?

REGENERATING LOVE

CHAPTER FIVE

1. Explain how man may use his creative forces in co-operation with the creative law.

2. What are the "sons of God" in Scripture symbology?

3. How do we know that Being is masculine and feminine?

4. What is the name and nature of God's most beautiful "daughter"?

5. Name some virtues and vices of mother love.

6. Explain love in its role of "gravity."

7. Is love ever a source of misery? Explain.

8. Give a remedy for divorce.

9. What do Adam, Eve, and the serpent symbolize in the individual?

10. Give the metaphysical explanation of Adam and Eve's eating of the fruit of the tree of the "knowledge of good and evil."

11. What place has love in the regeneration of man?

12. By what means can woman help to lift up man and free him from sense bondage?

13. Will incarnation cease when love is lifted up?

14. What was Jesus' mission on earth?

15. Where is the throne of love in man's spiritual body?

16. Who, among Jesus' disciples, personified love?

17. Give an original illustration of how unselfish love may be unfolded.

18. Should one employ force or suppression in soul unfoldment? Why?

QUESTION HELPS

POWER—DOMINION—MASTERY

CHAPTER SIX

1. What is essential to the realization and demonstration of spiritual power?

2. Over what should man exercise his divine birthright of power?

3. Locate the throne of power in man's body consciousness, and tell what disciple of Jesus represents power.

4. What effect has development of power on the voice?

5. How and to what extent are one's words imbued with power?

6. Can we overcome the belief in limited or declining power? How?

7. Should man develop power before he overthrows carnal selfishness in himself? Why?

8. How can we distinguish between right and wrong in the use of our power?

9. What is the key to the exercising of dominion successfully in the material world and the restoring of equilibrium between Spirit and matter?

10. What rule laid down by Jesus is the basis of world peace and prosperity?

11. When will the "new heaven and . . . new earth" appear?

12. What is involved in overcoming the world, the flesh, the devil, and even death?

13. What is the devil?

14. Give the metaphysical interpretation of the Crucifixion.

15. What is the acme of man's power and dominion?

THE WORK OF THE IMAGINATION IN
REGENERATION

CHAPTER SEVEN

1. What is the imagination?
2. What disciple of Jesus represents the imagination?
3. Within man what office has the imaging faculty?
4. Why were Jesus' ideas so powerful and enduring?
5. What is the key to the interpretation of symbols?
6. What determines the character of soul and body?
7. Do dreams and visions play an important part in man's soul development? Explain why, and give Scripture examples.
8. Interpret spiritually Peter's vision, which is described in the 10th chapter of Acts.
9. What does man's body represent? Explain why.
10. Why do individuals and nations sometimes revert from culture to savagery?
11. How should man handle the animal propensities in himself?
12. Does the fact that animals are good in their rightful place justify man's using them for food? Why?
13. How was the original creation given character and form?
14. What, potentially, are animals?
15. When will animals cease to be in the objective?

UNDERSTANDING

CHAPTER EIGHT

1. Do *wisdom, understanding, knowledge,* and *intelligence* all mean the same thing?
2. Explain the two great realms of mind.
3. Was Jesus scientific in His teaching?

4. What faculty of mind is given first place by those who have spiritual discernment?

5. What phase of mind comes first in soul development?

6. What does Solomon stand for?

7. What did the Lord also give unto Solomon because He was so well pleased with him?

8. What part does the heart play in soul unfoldment?

9. Why do we have to be careful in distinguishing between true inspiration and our intellectual reasoning?

10. What does John the Baptist stand for in man's consciousness?

11. Who did Jesus say John the Baptist had been?

12. What takes place in man when he gives himself wholly unto the Lord?

13. Explain the relationship between John the Baptist and Jesus.

14. How does this relationship apply to man's consciousness?

15. What is the greatest of all the powers of man?

16. Do all the faculties enter into the regeneration of man?

17. Does man have the privilege of attaining eternal life?

THE WILL IS THE MAN

CHAPTER NINE

1. What faculty of mind is the motive power for all the other faculties?

2. What other faculty is most closely related to it?

3. What part does the imagination play in the development of the soul?

4. Why has man been given free will?

5. What is the work of the solar plexus?

6. How do the will and the understanding conflict in the expression of the spiritual life?

7. What causes hardening of the arteries?

8. Where does "motive" come in?

9. Explain what is meant by man's partaking of the knowledge of good and evil.

10. What does Jesus represent in soul development?

11. How does the Christ discipline His disciples (faculties)?

12. Explain how the will is often allowed to become destructive.

13. What is the will of Divine Mind for man as regards his actions?

14. Explain why a person should be positive in submitting his will to the authority of God instead of doing so in a negative way.

15. With what power and authority did Jesus endow His disciples to go forth and preach?

16. Does God's will for man change?

17. Why do sin, sickness, suffering, and death come into man's life?

18. Should a person submit his will to the control of another? Explain.

19. How should a person make his affirmations?

20. Give the words of Jesus that may be used as an affirmation in bringing about relaxation, peace, and harmony.

SPIRITUAL LAW AND ORDER

CHAPTER TEN

1. For what did Jesus denounce the scribes and Pharisees?

2. Should teachers or leaders frame rules of thought and action for their members? Why?

3. What did Jesus lay down as the only safe foundation for all religious work?

4. Why did Jesus break the Mosaic law?

5. What does the Sabbath day stand for in man's consciousness?

6. Explain why Jesus said that He came not to break the law, but to fulfill it.

7. Why must man erase from his mind all authority and tradition of other men in order to fulfill God's will for him?

8. What place have sacred writings in man's life?

9. What is the only authority?

10. Shall we leave our fellows free to worship God as they see fit, and to what extent do we co-operate with them?

11. Where does man find real communion with the Father?

12. What part does Jesus, the "only begotten Son" of God, play in man's unfoldment?

13. What does Moses' fleeing to the wilderness represent in man's consciousness? Explain.

14. What gives our words and thoughts power to accomplish that whereto they are sent?

15. What forces do Moses and Pharaoh represent? Explain.

16. Explain the place of denial and affirmation in man's growth.

ZEAL—ENTHUSIASM

CHAPTER ELEVEN

1. What is the function of the ego in forming mental states of consciousness? Explain.

2. What is zeal?

3. Can the divine law be broken? Explain.

4. Should one suppress the impulse of zeal that wells up in consciousness?

5. Why is it necessary for zeal to be tempered with wisdom?

6. How do one's different combinations of thoughts affect soul and body?

7. What is the meaning of the name "Simon Peter"? What is the meaning of the name "Simon, the Cananæan"?

8. Explain how the vitamins in the food that we eat are stored up in body consciousness and liberated.

9. Has zeal any part to play in one's becoming a genius along any line of endeavor?

10. Explain Jesus' words, "The very hairs of your head are numbered."

11. Explain Emerson's words, "Be not deceived by dimples and curls; that child is a thousand years old."

12. How do you account for Mozart's wonderful ability to play the organ without instruction at the age of four years?

13. Where does the zeal center have its throne of dominion?

RENUNCIATION

CHAPTER TWELVE

1. What is the first step in experiencing conversion?

2. Explain the effect of a change of mind upon the body organism.

3. In the process of body renewal, where does renunciation come in?

4. How does the metaphysician arrive at his conclusions concerning mind action?

5. State one big fundamental truth brought out in the study of mind.

6. Explain the distinction between the realm of ideas and the realm of thought.

7. Explain how thoughts are assimilated by the mind.

8. How does the mind act upon the body?

9. Why should wisdom be exercised in the control of the mind?

10. Should man be given his freedom? Explain.

11. How are traits of mind and body handed down from generation to generation?

12. How are these dissolved in memory?

13. Explain medical science's method of combating disease germs.

14. Why has it failed?

15. What is the one healing power? Explain its action.

16. Describe the work of the disciple Thaddaeus.

17. What is the cause of constipation? of tumors? of the slowing down of the life forces?

18. What is the cause of adenoids? of inflamed tonsils? of sinus trouble?

19. How may these ills be avoided?

GENERATIVE LIFE

CHAPTER THIRTEEN

1. What is the life energy?

2. Is life intelligent? Explain.

3. Why is the life ego called the "adversary"?

4. Why are sensation and generation necessary to man's character? Explain.

5. What is the Son of man?

6. What does the Garden of Eden symbolize?

7. Upon what does the bringing forth of the ideal man depend?

8. What three factors enter into every consciousness?

9. What is the Lamb of God? Explain.

10. What is symbolized by the "river of water of life"?

11. Wherein comes the danger in experiencing this holy stream of life?

12. How are bodily sensations lawfully experienced? Explain.

13. Why is it necessary to cleanse this pure stream of life in its flow outward?

14. Explain: "As Moses lifted up the serpent in the wilderness, even so must the Son of man be lifted up."

15. Explain sensation's being a divine creation.

16. How is all intemperance overcome?

17. Explain your being "dead through your trespasses and sins."

INDEX

INDEX

PRINTED IN U. S. A.

37C-5M-2-41